Response to Failure

American University Studies

Series IV
English Language and Literature

Vol. 169

PETER LANG
New York • Washington, D.C./Baltimore • Boston
Bern • Frankfurt am Main • Berlin • Vienna • Paris

Pushpa Naidu Parekh

Response to Failure

Poetry of Gerard Manley Hopkins, Francis Thompson, Lionel Johnson, and Dylan Thomas

PETER LANG
New York • Washington, D.C./Baltimore • Boston
Bern • Frankfurt am Main • Berlin • Vienna • Paris

Library of Congress Cataloging-in-Publication Data

Parekh, Pushpa Naidu.
Response to failure: poetry of Gerard Manley Hopkins,
Francis Thompson, Lionel Johnson, and Dylan Thomas / Pushpa Naidu Parekh.
  p. cm. — (American university studies. Series IV,
English language and literature; vol. 169)
Includes bibliographical references.
1. English poetry—19th century—History and criticism. 2. Failure
(Psychology) in literature. 3. Hopkins, Gerard Manley, 1844–1889—
Knowledge—Psychology. 4. Johnson, Lionel Pigot, 1867–1902—Knowledge—
Psychology. 5. Thompson, Francis, 1859–1907—Knowledge—Psychology.
6. Thomas, Dylan, 1914–1953—Knowledge—Psychology. I. Title. II. Series.
  PR595.F34P37   821'.809—dc20   93-18360
           ISBN 0-8204-2152-9
           ISSN 0741-0700

Die Deutsche Bibliothek-CIP-Einheitsaufnahme

Parekh, Pushpa Naidu:
Response to failure: poetry of Gerard Manley Hopkins,
Francis Thompson, Lionel Johnson, and Dylan Thomas /
Pushpa Naidu Parekh. –New York; Boston; Washington, D.C./Baltimore; Boston;
Bern; Frankfurt am Main; Berlin; Vienna; Paris: Lang.
(American university studies: Ser. 4, English language and literature; Vol. 169)
           ISBN 0-8204-2152-9
       NE: American university studies / 04

Cover design by Andy Ruggirello.
Cover Photo, *A New Perspective,* by Dr. Bharat S. Parekh.

The paper in this book meets the guidelines for permanence and durability
of the Committee on Production Guidelines for Book Longevity
of the Council of Library Resources.

© 1998 Pushpa Naidu Parekh

All rights reserved.
Reprint or reproduction, even partially, in all forms such as microfilm,
xerography, microfiche, microcard, and offset strictly prohibited.

Printed in the United States of America.

Dedication

To my loving husband, Bharat
and my adorable daughter, Shruti

"Man's spirit will be flesh-bound when found at best,
But unencumberèd"

Gerard Manley Hopkins
"The Caged Skylark"

Acknowledgments

I wish to acknowledge with thanks permission granted to reproduce in this volume the following material:

Quotes from Gerard Manley Hopkins, *The Poems of Gerard Manley Hopkins,* 4th ed. (1970), edited by W. H. Gardner and N. H. Mackenzie. London, New York: Oxford University Press. By permission of Oxford University Press.

Quotes from Lionel Johnson, *The Collected Poems of Lionel Johnson,* 2nd and revised edition (1982), edited by Ian Fletcher. Hamden, CT: Garland Publishing. By permission of Garland Publishing.

Quotes from Dylan Thomas, *The Collected Poems of Dylan Thomas 1934-1952* (1957), *The Collected Stories* (1971), and *Under Milk Wood: A Play for Voices* (1954). New York: New Directions Publishing. By permission of New Directions Publishing.

Quotes from Francis Thompson, *Francis Thompson: Poems and Essays, Three Volumes in One* (1947), edited by Wilfred Meynell. The Newman Bookshop. No copyright renewal.

Front cover photograph, *"A new perspective,"* by permission of Bharat S. Parekh.

This book was made possible by the loving support, encouragement and enthusiasm of the following people:

Drs. Donald E. Stanford and Rebecca Crump who helped me, through my graduate years, to formulate and express my thoughts and concepts central to the book.

Dr. Norman Friedman for his generosity in reading the manuscript and commenting on it.

Drs. Michael Allsopp and Desmond Egan of the Gerard Manley Hopkins Society Annual International Summer School for their support of my scholarship.

Dr. Johnetta Cole, the President, Dr. Glenda Price, the provost, and the Faculty Development Committee, Spelman College, for providing grant-support during the preparation of the book and Dr. Cole and the Scholarship and Awards Committee for honoring me with the Presidential Faculty Award for Scholarly Achievement, 1996.

Ms. Heidi Burns and Ms. Lisa Dillon of Peter Lang for their support and directions in finalizing the book.

Dr. C. T. Indra of University of Madras, India, for inspiring me with her passion for literature and encouraging me to publish.

My friends and colleagues in the English Department and the African Diaspora and the World, Spelman College, for their unstinting interest in my work.

My dear parents, Mr. and Mrs. Naidu and my special sisters, Ajanta and Madhu, and their beautiful families for their prayers, love and encouragement.

My husband, Bharat and my daughter, Shruti for their wholesome love, their total involvement in all my pursuits, and their generosity and patience in giving me time and space to work on this book.

Table of Contents

Introduction 1

Chapter 1. "The War Within": Gerard Manley Hopkins, the Poet-Priest 11

Chapter 2. The Self and the Other: Response to Failure in Communication 37

Chapter 3. Between the Miraculous and the Quotidian: Francis Thompson, the Visionary Poet 65

Chapter 4. Lionel Johnson and the Aesthetics of Failure in Fin de Siècle 99

Chapter 5. The Clown's Grimace: Dylan Thomas and Response to Failure of Modern Man 143

Conclusion 175

Bibliography 183

Introduction

i

The present study, a considerably revised and updated version of my doctoral dissertation, explores the possibilities of understanding the texture of autobiographical experiences that inform the poems, as well as of applying Reader-Response and Culture Studies theories to analyze and evaluate their effects today among reading communities that seem to reflect the problematics of our global societies. At times seemingly secular, multicultural and often egalitarian, these communities have evolved with world phenomena such as transculturism and transnationalism and also exhibit resurgence of religious revivalism, cultural factionalism, ethnic chauvenism, and increasing economic inequities. They also often vocalize the tensions within these emerging dialogics, as is apparent in the surfacing of nationalistic sentiments, politically divisive borders and neo-colonial hegemonies. How do readers today respond to writers who have traditionally been studied within the defined parameters of traditionally male dominated Euro-American canons? The fear of many supporters of "Canonical Literature" in our academia impinges on an almost post-modern anxiety of displaced territorial defence and preservation in the face of what seems like an increasingly aggressive "encroachment" of not merely Feminism, but an openly "third world" Feminism and of culture studies such as Post-Colonialism. On the other hand, current critical endeavors in breaking paradigms of academic politics and power struggles have scarcely encouraged re-reading the "Canonical" literature in ways that clarify the links between what is read, who reads them, where, when, why and how. My interest in both areas of study lies in creating and integrating a methodology that allows for exchange and interchange between the so-called "center" and the "margin."

My study brings together a number of traditional and non-traditional readings to examine the works of four male European (mainly Anglo) writers whose works are very often studied within the limited scope of

Victorianism or Modernism, somehow distancing them from our supposedly post-modern or even post post-modern societies and reading communities. My attempt here is to re-study these poets within the historical, biographical as well as present reader-centered socio-cultural and often political realities. In this light, Hopkins' inner "warfare" is relevant to not only Tractarians or New Critics but to Feminists as well, Thompson and Johnson's life and art reveal the personal as well as the age's concerns with expressions of class as well as political imperialism, and finally Thomas with his constant double awareness of national and cultural borders, the Anglo-Welsh identity, is a figure that is as relevant as Yeats in our present culture-studies approaches to literature.

In studying them, one understands their relevance to today's writers and readers, without glorifying a hierarchized system, so that studying Anglo-British writers alongwith postcolonial or women writers creates no simple oppositions of race, gender and cultural ideology, but poses their interactive relationships as complex but realistic in today's global societies.

ii

The study of the response to failure as reflected in the poems of Hopkins, Thompson, Johnson and Thomas, implies two levels of responses, including the reader's response to one aspect of the textual structure, that is, the experience of the persona as actualized in the selected poems. I will retain this New Critical term "persona" with all its dramatic and rhetorical implications but extend its scope as it interacts with a reader's persona, a projection of the reading self in a certain defined role. The experience of the persona under study itself constitutes one of failure and response to failure. Thus, the reader is involved in a double activity: responding to the experience of reading and concretizing the experience of the poetic persona's response to failure in the reading process. The interrelationships among the poet, the text, and the reader are my area of investigation. In the process I utilize the poets' biographical and autobiographical materials as well as consider the social, psychological and historical forces affecting the text and the reader's response as influential factors. The theory of "transaction," a balanced approach to literary works, as suggested by Louise M. Rosenblatt in *The Reader, the Text, the Poem*, is the emphasis in the present study. Rosenblatt clearly places this approach within the historical span of literary criticism:

> Within the past few years, the spotlight has started to move in the direction of the reader. Sometimes the reaction has been more against the social-political implications of the New Criticism than against its aesthetic theory. Sometimes the rehabilitation of the reader takes the form of a rather extreme subjectivism or Freudianism. Thus, some, preoccupied with the author's text, have seen the reader as a tabula rasa, receiving the imprint of "the poem." Others, in reaction, see the text as empty, awaiting the context brought by the reader. Rejecting both of these extremes, the discussion that follows begins with readers encountering a text and proceeds to meet the basic questions that flow from this event. The purpose will be to admit into the limelight the whole scene—author, text, and reader. We shall be especially concerned with the member of the cast who has hitherto been neglected—the reader. (4-5)[1]

Emphasis on the reader also involves an understanding of what Gayatri Chakravorty Spivak in *In Other Worlds: Essays in Cultural Politics* refers to as "our own elusive historico-politico-economico-sexual determination" (28). Edward Said in *The World, the Text, and the Critic* describes the text's "worldliness":

> Texts have ways of existing, both theoretical and practical, that even in their most rarefied form are always enmeshed in circumstance, time, place, and society—in short, they are in the world, and hence are worldly. (35)

Refuting arguments for limitlessness of interpretation, Said articulates the reader's role as that of engaging in "complementary, as opposed to supplementary reading" (39). Said's example, in particular of Hopkins, is of significance in that it underscores the boundaries within which author-text-reader interactions produce meaning:

> Modern literary history gives us a number of writers whose text, as a text, incorporates quite explicitly the circumstances of its very concretely imagined, and even described, situation. One type of author, exemplified by Hopkins, Wilde, and Conrad—conceives his text as supported explicitly by a discursive situation involving speaker and audience; the designed interplay between speech and reception, between verbal-/ity and textuality *is* the text's situation, its placing itself in the world. (40)

The text, besides being an imagined construct, places itself both in the world of the author as well as that of the reader. The author's experiences as well as his "in-experiences" in his world find either direct or indirect expression, but also often find alternative projections through "masks" or personae. These expressions and projections, in my study, are narrowed down to the realm of the selected poets' experiences of failure. Each of the poets selected in the present study experienced a sense of failure in his personal life or in his relation to the external world, and responded to it with extreme sensitivity. The concern here is with the experience actualized in the poems as that of the persona, and with comparing and contrasting it with the poet's experience in life. But since the poet disappears from the poems as a poet, the emphasis is on what is accessible to the reader, that is, the poem itself and the personality within the poem: the persona, his experiences and responses arising out of a nexus of social, personal and psychological conditions implied in the poem itself. Some of the persona's experiences can be summed up as follows: the persona's involvement in a struggle between a personal and a social interpretation of what constitutes a failure; resistance to and acceptance of the role of failure (reflected in the persona of a failed artist, a disappointed believer, a thwarted lover, a lonely exile, a cynical sceptic or a bumbling clown); the persona's attempts at actualizing self-integration (as in Hopkins, Thompson and Johnson) and his attempts at emphasizing his own alienation and disintegration in the loss of a "containing framework," as in Thomas and the moderns (Barrett 35).

Some of the ensuing relationships between the reader's response and the text can be summed up as follows: empathy/antipathy between the persona's response to the experience of failure and the value system of the reader growing out of his/her particular conditions (such as those of time and place) which define and focus his/her understanding of aesthetic experiences in a certain direction; moments of contact and of breaks in contact between the reader and the experiencing persona in the poem traced to underlying motivations; the interaction of the mask of the persona and that of the reader in the context of trying out or breaking role-models. The production of meaning thus becomes not only the product but also the process involved in the "performance" of reading, as Edward Said explains in relation to Hopkins' poetry:

> This dialectics of production is everywhere present in Hopkins's work. Writing is telling; nature is telling; reading is telling....So close is the identification in Hopkins's mind between world, word, and the utterance, the three coming alive together as a moment of performance, that here is no need of critical intervention. (41)

While Said rightfully claims "It is the written word that provides the immediate circumstantial reality for the poem's 'play'" (41), it is the reader's act of reading that realizes its performance. In "A Reader's Life: Selving Through Reading Hopkins," David Anthony Downes refers to Paul Ricocur's "hermeneutics of selving" and his own experience in reading Hopkins: "His (Hopkins') poetry came across more as speech than writing. Poetic sentence by poetic sentence enacted a voice talking to me about something powerfully intending. Reading his writing demanded a speech reenactment."[2] Selving, for the reader, becomes a "living drama" in which he is "partly dramatist and partly actor" (340). In his latest work *Hopkins Achieved Self*, Downes focuses on analyzing this "central phenomenological component of Hopkins' writings" in order to link Hopkins' selving as a hermeneutic act of "self-texting" and self-transformation with the reader's selving, the "meaning-making state of the reader who inspires the text into a personal life meaning."[3]

The task of relating the poetic experiences derived from one poet to the other involves the task of comparing and contrasting but also synthesizing the kind of activities the personae as well as the readers are involved in during the reading experience. The accessibility of the work to the individual reader is determined not only by the reader's interaction with the core of the textual structure and its various stratifications (inclusive of what Roman Ingardin explores, on the levels of sound, image and vocabulary), but also by the motivations of the persona underlying his projection of self and his experience. In some of the poems, the persona through extravagant diction, language and imagery desires the reader's distance from his experience; in others, he builds up a rapport with the reader by drawing him/her in through simple, direct, evocative language and by assigning him/her the role of a participant. The reader responds by accepting, rejecting, or modifying the assigned role, or by discovering a new role and developing a new structure of responses. The interaction with the reader implies failure or success in communication on other levels too—between the persona and the remote, often inaccessible God, between the hapless lover and his spiritualized beloved, between the alienated subject and his political and cultural reality, between the comic-pathetic self and the creative-destructive universe.

An area of investigation specifically relevant to the selected poets in this study is that of Feminism. The late nineteenth century, especially the fin de siècle period, has been re-read by feminist critics in a way that places the articulation of sexual and gender anomalies in Hopkins, the aesthetes and the male modernists in a new light. Linda Dowling's early essay "The Decadent and the New Woman" , Bram Dijkstra's *Idols of Perversity: Fantasies of Feminine Evil in Fin de Siècle Culture*, Sandra M. Gilbert and Susan Gubar's *Sexchanges, No Man's Land: The Place of the Woman Writer in the Twentieth Century,* and *Madwoman in the Attic,* Cynthia Eagle Russett's *Sexual Science: The Victorian Construction of Womanhood,* and Elaine Showalter's *Sexual Anarchy: Gender and Culture at the Fin de Siècle* and *Daughters of Decadence* are influential works that have been published since 1979. These works provide not only new sites of author-text-reader interaction but also enable explorations into the socio-political circumstances that create barriers or bridges in this interaction.

Moreover, in this study I have actively incorporated significant material derived from neo-historical and culture-studies perspectives, especially those dealing with issues of colonization and decolonization. The relationship of author, text and reader to their world/s is a complex one, no doubt, but one in which the historical reality of one's time, place and culture defines and shapes one's conception of self-identity and performance—crucial issues in examining the selected poet's struggles with the experience of failure at various personal, social, political and artistic levels. Further, in exemplifying the late twentieth century reader (often categorically assumed to be a Western reader with certain shared notions of cultural beliefs and experiences), one must grapple with a "multicultural" reader (after all, we are talking of global societies in practically every area; critics in literary studies need to actively address and explode the myth of a culturally monolithic reading public). In such a global society, the reader's role or even position as a reader may often reflect his/her self-devised and socially assigned place, which itself is in the process of being defined. In this context, Stanley Fish's definition of "reading communities" as "interpretive communities" poses the problematics of shared versus contested terrains of cultural experience.[4] What responses do Hopkins' feminine persona or Thompsons' rhetoric of Britannica, Johnson and the decadent's emphasis on male friendships as well as the politics of their "apolitical" aesthetics evoke? How do we respond to Dylan Thomas' ambiguous sympathy for Wales and Ireland while writing in English? In a time when imperialism and colonization are subjects of critical evaluation, how do readers from previously colonized worlds read and respond to the tensions in the Anglo poets' personal experiences of failure and the Empire's insistence on creating an image of its "success" through a literature in support of colonial agendas? The various references to "battles" and "warfares" that resound in late nineteenth century and poets of the World War era, though with a marked change in sensibility, evoke questions regarding the politics of the author's, the text's and the reader's worlds. These questions become foregrounded to readers who have been influenced, especially in the last two decades, by the discourses of deconstruction, neo-historicism, gender and culture studies. Of special significance in this area are studies published since 1980, such as Chinweizu, et al., *Toward the Decolonization of African Literature*, a response to it by Emeka Okeke-Ezigbo in "The 'Sharp and Sided Hail': Hopkins and his Nigerian Imitators and Detractors" in *Hopkins Among the Poets*, as well as *Decolonizing Tradition: New Views of Twentieth Century "British" Literary Canons*, edited by Karen R. Lawrence and Chris Bongie's *Exotic Memories: Literature, Colonialism and the Fin de Siècle*.[5]

Synthesizing and linking the various chapters in my book has involved me in a process of inquiry into the layered, sometimes co-existent, selves of the poets as well as myself as reader. In this light, it is important to clarify that the present study is not concerned with debates or speculations regarding whether the poets were "failures" or not; it is concerned with responding to poems dealing with highly self-conscious personae who enact their belief that their responses to the experience of failure reflect useful and relevant means of structuring experience, even if the experience is unsatisfactory. In one sense, this study decolonizes the subject-object relationship of authors-texts-readers. In placing the reader within apparently discordant realities of the aesthetics and the politics of literary production, I attempt to secure neither defensive platforms for "canonical" writers nor unexamined support for recent currents in oppositional discourses. I only envision the complexity of our impinging multi-cultural worlds in ways that makes reading literature an exciting feat of the mind, heart and soul, as well as an engagement of one's politics, experiences and spiritual convictions.

Notes

1. Several critics have dealt with the notion of historical and implied authors and readers, chief among them being Wayne C. Booth and Wolfgang Iser. Booth in *The Rhetoric of Fiction*, second edition (Chicago: University of Chicago Press, 1983) uses the following terms: "Flesh-and-Blood" authors and audiences; "implied author" and "postulated reader" ; "The Teller of this Tale" and the "Credulous Listener" ; " The Career-Author" and the "Career-Reader" ; and "Super-Author" and "the Reading Public." Iser in *The Act of Reading: A Theory of Aesthetic Response* (Baltimore: Johns Hopkins University Press, 1978), refers to a "transcendental model" and a "phenomenological reader," (38, 34) and in *The Implied Reader: Patterns of Communication in Prose Fiction from Bunyan to Becket* (Baltimore: John Hopkins University Press, 1974), Iser defines "the implied reader": "The term incorporates both the prestructuring of the potential meaning by the text, and the reader's actualization of this potential through the reading process" (xii). William Nelles in "Historical and Implied Authors and Readers," in *Comparative Literature* 45.1 (1993): 22-47, provides a critical discussion of the usage of the terminology.

2. David Anthony Downes, "A Reader's Life: Selving through Reading Hopkins" *Saving Beauty: Further Studies in Hopkins,* eds. Michael L. Allsopp and David Anthony Downes. New York: Garland, 1994, 333 .

3. David Anthony Downes, *Hopkins' Achieved Self* (Lanham, Maryland: University Press of Amercia, 1996) 5.

4. Stanley Fish in *Is There a Text in This Class? The Authority of Interpretive Communities* (Cambridge, Mass.: Harvard University Press, 1980) focuses on the conventions of interpretive communities as solely contributing to interpretations of texts. Robert C. Holub in *Reception Theory: A Critical Introduction* (New York: Methuen, 1984) poses a relevant criticism of Fish's metacritical assumptions: "The apparent stability of views on some texts or on the fact that texts are stable may be the consequence of membership in a cohesive interpretive coterie, but where does this group's stability originate, and how can it be defined and determined? The text may indeed disappear in Fish's model, but determinacy simply crops up in another guise. Even if we agree that nothing belongs to the text, that it is ultimately not describable, as soon as we register similarity of interpretation, we are bound to admit something determinate, controlling our agreement in interpretation" (151-152).

5. Chinweizu, et al, in *Toward the Decolonization of African Literature* (Enugu, Nigeria:

Fourth Dimension Publishers, 1980) are critical of the negative influences of Hopkins and Western modernists, on Nigerian writers, referring to this influence as the "Hopkins Disease." Emeka Okeke-Ezigbo in "The 'Sharp and Sided Hail': Hopkins and his Nigerian Imitators and Detractors," in *Hopkins Among the Poets: Studies in Modern Responses to Gerard Manley Hopkins*, ed. Richard F. Giles (Hamilton, Ontario: The International Hopkins Association, 1985) addresses the "*international popularity*" and "*cult*" status of Hopkins (114) and the influence of other Western models on Nigerian writers and counters the "Hopkins Disease" as the unfortunate result of "literary plunder" : "Indeed, Hopkins could have helped the circumspect Nigerian writer to be more African, in the sense that Hopkins's idea of *inscape* implies that every created thing has its own *raison d'etre*" (121).

Chapter 1

"The War Within": Gerard Manley Hopkins, the Poet-Priest[1]

Gerard Manley Hopkins aimed at inscaping nature, God and man in his poetry. Yet despite this central unity and pattern, his poetry records a strikingly never-ceasing whirl of activity, process and creactivity reflective of Hopkins' own life. The whole is always seething with the fragmented parts and it is this condition of continual "breaking within" that Hopkins' poetry captures. Often, Hopkins' inscape is considered to be the mark of the individual, its unity and pattern; yet Hopkins' poetry, especially the later poetry, rings with a perception of fragments, of pieces and parts not always coinciding or unifying with each other. His "inscape" seems to celebrate, beyond the unity and pattern of the individual being, the very existence of the duality, even the multiplicity of the individual being's nature. This duality or multiplicity is not always is opposition or contradiction, but neither is it in total conformity. Rather, the whole (a cognizable self) is the burgeoning of the fragmented parts (the self-divisions and the different roles of the persona in the poems) into a shape recognizable by the reader. Inscape, then, implies the interaction, the chiasmas between the whole and the fragmented, chaotic parts of the individual being. "Inscape" is the final recognizable shape of the experiencing self and also the product of the reader's consistency-building activity. In *The Act of Reading*, Wolfgang Iser describes this activity as "a Basis for Involvement in the Text as an Event"; it involves the reader's "continual modification of memory and increasing complexity of expectation" leading to a "synthesizing acitivity" (118-119).[2] "Instress," as an effect in Hopkins' poetry, is the impact on the perceiver (the persona and the reader) of this never-ceasing whirl of activity, of the transferring over of the parts to the whole and the whole to the parts, a process of eternal giving and taking within the being and between the self and the world without.

This understanding of inscape and instress attempts to construct a meaningful bridge among Hopkins' poetry, his life and the act of reading. Through such a perception, the fragmented life of Hopkins as a priest, poet and man is seen not as a mere contradiction, though he often felt it as such. Alhough he experienced these roles as hurtling against each other, they can be viewed as involvement in a process or even the necessary tensions in the evolution of a self-other dynamic. Not all the collisions of the parts are fruitful but, nevertheless, the whole takes a shape from the chiasmas of the parts. It is this eternal giving and taking process which is evident in his poetry and when we put them together we, as readers, begin to recognize the shape of Hopkins' poetic output. While the priest-persona gave up the sensuality and fecundity of life, the persona as poet demanded it; what the poet sometimes doubted and despaired in (kindly love of God), the persona as priest affirmed and rejoiced in. Though we can still say that inscape is the pattern of the individual being, we need to comprehend that pattern here is not a static, given quality; rather, it is an evolving shape. It is the intrinsic interplay of the parts among themselves and the whole as it is emerging into shape. This is what is called the "selving" of the individual being. Hopkins, in recording the fragmented parts of his self, was recording the very process of inscaping the whole, the final shape of his own individual being. In addition, the reader performs his own "selving" act as well, by responding to the recurring and differing roles of the persona at the experimental core of the poems. In his essay titled "A Reader's Life: Selving Through Reading Hopkins," which appeared in *Saving Beauty*, David A. Downes refers to the "hermeneutics of selving" both in the poet and the reader as an act of self-dramatization and "self-texting."[2]

The consciousness of self-fragmentation and, consequently, the need to define the selving process all the more intensely is actualized not only in the persona's struggle with his experience but also in the reader's response to the persona, projected at several sites of achievement and failure, particularly in the two vocations of priesthood and poetic writing. This dual nature of the persona's sense of failure does not necessarily mean Hopkins conceived of his two vocations as being contradictory or self-exclusive. Rather, these two roles both formed the wholeness of his selfhood. What he recorded in his works was not so much a clash between the two vocations but an emergence of each in a specifically intrinsic way. Besides the call of duty and the kinds of work involved, each vocation affected the other in a certain way. Hopkins would probably never have realized a wholeness of self if he had devoted himself to only one vocation. Neither, paradoxically, did he find a satisfying complement of the poet/priest vocations. Instead of building on this dichotomy which has been elaborated on and discussed several times before, this chapter will concentrate on the persona in Hopkins' poems as he responds to his failures in the two vocations and their effect on the reader, the reader's involvement in the outcome of the poem, and the parallels and divergences between Hopkins and the evolving persona in their roles of poet and priest.

Our response, as readers, to the poet-priest persona in Hopkin's poems involves a dynamic, often a self-corrective process. This process can be illustrated by focusing on one aspect of the priest's confrontation with the possibility of failure in his chosen vocation: the struggle between human desires and their sacrifice in an ascetic way of life. In the early poems, the priest-persona responds to any signs of physical or sexual awareness in himself with fierce loathing and intense shame, often expressed as a desire to hide. In "Poem 16" and "Poem 18," the persona's awareness of the self's sinfulness is never concretized.[4] It is a rather overwhelming, generalized sinfulness from the specific nature of which the persona attempts to hide. His response to the sense of sinfulness of self is scattered through the very process of generalizing the sin. By failing to specify the sinfulness, the persona is building his own world of delusions even as he seems psychologically to disperse the strength and force of the guilt he felt so severely. The evasiveness of the persona triggers off an image-forming action on the part of the reader. The persona's self-delusions take force in a situation that is slowly built up as the reader forms her/his images—the dual situation where the persona is alone, confronting himself as in a soliloquy and one in which he is keenly aware of himself and his audience like a self-conscious performer on stage. This situation-building is the reader's actualization of the persona's dilemma, the conflict between inner desire (sexual, sensual or worldly ambition) and outer norm (social and vocational). Wolfgang Iser in *The Act of Reading* points out that "fictional language provides instructions for the building of a situation and so for the production of an imaginary object" (64). This process of situation-building on the part of the reader reflects her/his own process of interpretation of what is being signified or suggested as she/he plays out certain roles. At first, as an outside, unacknowledged observer of the persona, she/he objectively traces the evasive generalizations in the persona's self-accusations, and contrasts them with the otherwise specific details in the poems. But soon, the reader becomes aware of the persona's self-consciousness and his addresses to a second person, figured as a patriarchal authority figure. The persona's audience is of course God, though he is never specifically mentioned; but in the reading process it is the reader who is the audience and also takes the position of the authority figure, however reluctantly. What was noticeable to an objective reader, the self-delusive nature of the persona, becomes all the more striking to the more discriminating reader as audience and as "God." Now the reader as a distinctly male authority figure, is in direct confrontation with the persona who places himself on a lower scale. The reader's response to the persona's ambiguities and evasive language and her/his own level of comfort at playing the role of audience as well as an authority figure, build up the emotional aura, the disposition with which she/he reacts to the persona. This kind of role-playing in a poetic context brings the reader and the persona into a tighter relationship than is experienced in reading Hopkins' own record of any signs of moral lapses in his diaries or even biographical analyses of Hopkins' feelings of guilt and self-torment. In the poetic context, the reader's evolving relationship with the persona is marked by a growing sense of emotional response, even though here it is one of antipathy, of a strained conflict of personalities and expectations, impying the various forms of master-servant relationships that define Hopkins' personal as well as public interactions with the icons of power, control and authority. The master-servant dichotomy expressed all the torment of unreconcilable forces for assertion as well as submission, which surprisingly evoked contradictory responses in his personae. They seem to desire submission, almost the erasure of a self, yet they are so self-conscious, so scathingly self-aware.

In "Poem 18," the persona reverses his own self-delusive role and openly confesses to the hardening in himself, imaged as composed of iron and clay. Echoing "Deuteronomy" 28:23, "And thy heaven that is over thy head shall be brass, and the earth that is under thee shall be iron," the words reveal to the reader another aspect of the persona, his judgmental attitude to self.[5] The reader needs to go back and revise her/his sequence of image production to admit the persona's more complex personality, which is self-delusive at times, but also self-judgmental at other times. By the end of the poem, the reader is left with the persona's defiant words of waging war with God (27). The imagery of warfare and the ringing, heroic tone modify the reader's previous response to admit a growing impression of the youthfulness, almost the innocence of the persona in his confrontation with God.

In later poems, the persona is more explicit and less sexually anxious to express the "dangerous" attractiveness of the male physique, such as that of the sailor in "The Wreck of the Deutschland," Harry in "Harry Ploughman," the boy in "The Handsome Heart" and the lad in "The Bugler's First Communion." Each figure is celebrated in his physical activity. Steering clear of ambiguities in Hopkins' sexual responses, Wendall Stacey Johnson in "Sexuality and Inscape" points out a significant fact regarding Hopkins and sexuality:

> Yet Hopkins recognizes in his poetry, and recognized in his life, the power of sexuality as an intrinsic aspect of humanity and as an intensely attractive one. He knew about the charm and (for him) the moral danger of sexual beauty. On that subject he was not half-consciously or unconsciously repressed, not hypocritical. (65)[6]

Hopkins' recognition of his own sexual identity is dramatized in his personae's fluid gender roles. Alison Sulloway in "Hopkins, Male and Female, and the 'Tender Mothering Earth'," addresses the nature of "Hopkins' two archetypal gendered selves, the male and the female, in his priesthood and in his poetry" (34).[7] His "masculine" and "feminine archetypes," as Sulloway points out, find expression in a number of "paradigmatic patterns" such as : "male Jesuit," self as "Moses preaching in the wilderness and working in 'Christ's company' among God's warriors," as well as symbols of "pastoral world" as "mothering earth," "Mary, the virgin mother," self as "selfless nurse or mother, protecting his nurslings, individually or collectively, from sin's mortal stamp" (35). While God is visualized Father and masculine, Christ and Hopkins' self often occur in his poetry as androgynous. Placing this tendency in Hopkins within the Victorian cultural context, Sulloway argues, "Hopkins' permission to grant androgyny to himself and to other men but not to women, was entirely consistent with Victorian assumptions" (40).[8] Further Sulloway recognizes that undertaking male and female archetypal roles inevitably led to distress and "strain between the two types of functioning" (37). Evident in his personae are similar shifts in sexual identity. Sulloway examines Hopkins' Welsh poems, such as "God's Grandeur" in which "masculine outrage at industrial rapists of Victorian England" is linked with his own "maternal promptings" (40). In "The Windhover," which Sulloway describes as "full of benign paradoxes," the aggressive action of male achievement, "I caught," blends into the feminine withdrawal of "heart in hiding." Further, the image of self-sacrifice and humility of the feminine persona, hiding not only from the beauty of the windhover but his own receptivity to the inscapes of nature, undergoes transformation. The masculine self emerges and vocalizes the movement from self-denial and self-reticence to achievement and "mastery."

In the context of reader-response to the dynamic shifts occuring as the Hopkins' persona inscapes his masculine and feminine selves, one encounters quickly shifting scenarios in which the reader is drawn to concretize the outer and inner drama. Similarly, in "The Wreck of the Deutschland," the persona, in a whirl of masculine activity, hurtles between the ominous face of God and the impending force of Hell, to be stilled into the feminine moment of wonderment and adoration. The reader experiences language which reflects the inverted funnel structure of the tornado, both in physical nature and in human nature. While aural images through alliterations, assonance and onomatopoeia expand into the visual mouth of the funnel, the still point of the storm is symbolized in the failure of language, where words repeat and pauses break sounds into silence:

> The frown of his face
> Before me, the hurtle of hell
> Behind, where, where was a, where was a place? (52)

At the center of the last line, sound lingers on the short phonetic 'a,' symbolically expressive both of alphabetical beginning as well as the undefined mystery that it fails to articulate. The reader through the creation of aural and visual images must enact the profound vicissitudes of the persona's experience. Registering the pattern of shifting "masculine" and "feminine" uses of language, through sounds and images, the reader is drawn into the fluid 'gendering' of self experienced by the persona.

The reader's involvement now becomes much more intense and dynamic than ever before and the effect on him/her is of the density of the textual significations and the intensity of his/her own re-definitions and self-corrections which help to transform the text into a performance. Wolfgang Iser's analysis of the process of reader-response need not be limited to novels; the process he describes is actively realized in the more complex poems of Hopkins:

> Thus the reader's communication with the text is a dynamic process of self-correction, as he formulates signifieds which he must then continually modify. It is cybernetic in nature as it involves a feedback of effects and information throughout a sequence of changing situational frames; smaller units progressively merge into bigger ones, so that meaning gathers meaning in a kind of snowballing process. (67)

The significance of Hopkins' poetic expression of failure in vocation is worked out, however, not only in the dynamic relationship of the text and the reader but also in Hopkins' transformation of life experiences into art-experience. In his letter to Dixon, dated 12 October 1881, Hopkins elaborated on the attraction of an ascetic way of life, the priestly life, and the daily occupations and material concerns that detract one from this way (Abbott, ed., *Correspondence* 75-76).[9] In life, Hopkins felt pulled between the two vocations of priest and poet. He was to admit to Richard Dixon the "backward glances," the distractions and waste of time caused by his writing poetry and also the hopes of recognition aroused by it (83).

Another cause for disappointment and, in a sense, for a failing of the enthusiasm and fervency of his initial priestly duties, was the painfully overtaxing duties of teaching and examining students' papers. Not an outstanding teacher, Hopkins probably never enjoyed the lecturing and grading work, as they drained his energy to do anything else. In a letter to his mother, dated 20 April 1877, Hopkins described his work at St. Beuno's as a monotonous and tedious series of instructional activities and occasional priestly duties (Abbott, ed. *Further Letters* 148).[10] In his poetry, the sense of self's limitations is experienced as an ever-decreasing radius between the central self and the surrounding circumference. This effect is often achieved through the rhetorical use of repitition so that the locus of the self is repeatedly narrowed to a nothingness. In the poem "A Voice from the World," the persona echoes the self's journey in a limiting circle as the futility of travels that lead nowhere. Here, repetitions rise in a crescendo of negatives, "No flowers," "No colours," "No running," that converge to a point where the reader, struck by the verbal and structural repetition, responds to the ingathering process of the self, that is, the self's constant return to itself, imaged in terms of limitations both in movement and in experience. Hopkins' transformation of his life-experience into the persona's experience is marked by artistic control, a control achieved through the poetic development of the persona's restrained tone. In contrast to Hopkins' plaintive tone in his letters about burdensome priestly duties, the persona's appraisal is ambiguous. The self's journey is restricted by the surrounding circle, but nowhere does the self indicate whether the limiting circumference is the environment of the chosen vocation or the self's failure to actualize that which he seeks so intensely, that is, movement, expansion, and release from self-imprisonment.

Physical tiredness and weakness often caused Hopkins extreme anxiety and depression. In a letter to Baillie, dated 12 February 1868, Hopkins described his state of spiritual negation in an environment of depressing isolation and teaching overload (83). The reiteration of "no" (and its variants) after having said "yes" to the conversion is a self-conscious appraisal of self's failure. This self-consciousness, in his poetry, is a revealing characteristic of his persona, emphasized in the self-reflexive tone and the reiterations of "I," "My" and "me" in the "terrible sonnets," such as "No Worst there is None," "I Wake and Feel" and "My Own Heart." In these sonnets, however, the state of despair is not merely thrust on the persona. It results from the deadening of his senses and his inability to feel the inscapes he had described earlier, a state imaged as: "Selfyeast of spirit a dull dough sours." In ""Patience, hard thing" (Poem 68) the heightened sense of hearing the grating of hearts intensifies the persona's state of mind: he can "hear" but not "feel." In "My Own Heart" (Poem 69), spiritual barrenness is equated to physical blindness and thirst. Physical weakness or failure of the senses and emotional stultification play a major role in the persona's recording of his failures in spiritual aspiration. One explanation for this is given in the poem, "The Caged Skylark". The human body is not the spirit's prison but limitations of the body and the deadening of the senses and emotions, through the tedious drudgery of daily life, could encumber the spirit. In his letter to his mother, dated 30 April 1880, Hopkins expressed a similar sense of wretchedness of surroundings in Liverpool, during Easter week, and health problems related to over-work (Abbott, ed. *Further Letters*, 157). Similarly, he was disappointed with Dublin. In a letter to Bridges, dated 7 March 1884, Hopkins referred to Dublin as an inhospitable and polluted place (Abbott, ed. *The Letters*, 190).[11] In Hopkins' poems, however, the persona's expression of the limiting environment is mingled with a self-conscious awareness of his own limitations as well. Unlike the letters complaining about the priestly duties and environment, and unlike his early poems of masochistic self-blame, the mature poems of Hopkins show an artistic restraint. That is why these poems escape a purely self-confessional quality. They present a persona involved in an inner and an outer struggle (the self's struggle with itself and with its limiting environment). Both struggles achieve a psychological significance by the way the persona reveals and conceals his own personality, through choice of rhetorical devices, such as repetition of words, ambiguity of structure and tone of voice.

Consequently, the persona's evolving definition of the state of self as an exile is a recurring motif in Hopkins' poetry. In the fragment "Pilate," the persona feels "shut out" from Christ even as Pilate did. He is an exile in various senses of the word. Paradoxically, to the reader, the comparison between self's exile and that of Pilate seems almost self-deceiving. The persona's condition, ironically, is worse than Pilate's because, unlike Pilate, he feels "shut out" from Christ in the very vocation devoted to Christ. A similar sense of his physical exile is expressed in Hopkins' letter to Bridges, dated 26 July 1883, but without the paradox of self-knowledge and self-deception implicit in the persona-reader interaction of the poem. In this letter he views himself as "Fortune's football," constantly and aimlessly being displaced (183). Within the Jesuit order, Hopkins was made to move from place to place so that, as Paddy Kitchen notes, "binding attachments to place or person were never encouraged to develop" (145).[12] Though taking pride in "readiness for instant dispatch," "Hopkins viewed all these changes and the continual staff changes with a certain wryness" (145-146). Exile, for Hopkins, was a kind of death. In his sermons, Hopkins had related the political exile to banishment and the death of one's civil rights (Devlin, ed., 61, 165).[13] The Jesuit way of life, with its regular reassignment from place to place, often meant for Hopkins banishment from the comforts of family, friends and community. In contrast, the persona in "The Alchemist in the City" romantically celebrates self-banishment from the city to the wilderness in order to associate with the community of nature. Here is an early indication that the persona would never be satisfied without some kind of community, whether it be of nature, man or God. Through the willed act of self-banishment the persona, unlike the apathetic Hopkins of the letters, felt the need to find an alternative community to associate with.

On the other hand, within the Jesuit fold itself, Hopkins verged on a state of nervousness and crippling melancholy which debilitated him from acting independently. In one of his letters, Hopkins described this state as resembling madness (Abbott, ed., *Further Letters*, 256). Within a month, Hopkins wrote to Bridges on 17 May 1885, comparing his bouts of depression to a madness-like state (Abbott, ed., *The Letters*, 216). Though Hopkins was moved from place to place, the kind of work he had to do was the same. Hopkins' sense of failure in his religious vocation was heightened by his constant self-reminder (through diaries and letters) of the drudgery of institutional work which had no immediate or worthwhile results. In a letter to his mother, dated 5 July 1888, Hopkins wrote about his grading and teaching duties in Dublin that prevented him from doing any other fruitful work (Abbott, ed., *Further Letters* 184-185). In his "Retreat Notes," written at St. Stanislaus' College, Tullabeg, 1 January 1888, Hopkins emphasized the worthlessness of his work. Despondent at his own condition, he wrote:

> All my undertakings miscarry. I wish then for death: yet if I died now I should die imperfect, no master of myself and that is the worst failure of all. 0 my God, look

down on me. (Devlin, ed., 262)

His self-loathing persisted; almost two and a half months later he uses the same metaphor of barrenness, "Time's eunuch," to describe the poet-priest persona's condition in "Poem 74." Hopkins related his sense of despair to the kind of distress which led to suicide by a young medical student in their community. In a letter to Bridges, dated 7 September 1888, Hopkins despaired at ever getting relief from the exhaustion of mind and body:

> This reminds me of a shocking thing that has just happened to a young man well known to some of our community. He put his eyes out....After the deed he made his way to a cottage and said "I am blind please let me rest for an hour."... I mention the case because it is extraordinary: suicide is common. (Abbott, ed., *The Letters*, 282)

What does this juxtaposition of personal depression and suicidal attempts of others suggest? Besides the obvious combination of self-pity and self-condemnation, the links between the January and the September 1888 quotes are striking. In his "Retreat Notes," quoted above, Hopkins mentioned, "I am ashamed of the little I have done, of my waste of time" (Devlin, ed., 262). Eight months later, Hopkins suggested a connection between his despair and his disappointment over the nervous exhaustion of a medical student who put his eyes out so he could get rest. The sense of shame Hopkins felt in not having fulfilled the high achievements he had set for himself was also the underlying factor in his desire to hide. In the poems the persona hides from different embodiments of perfection: God, bird, and even his own inner self (for examples, see Hopkins 52, 69, 169). The idealized concept of the duties which Hopkins brought to his vocation was far from the reality of drudgery, isolation and monotony it involved. Consequently, Hopkins often felt discomfitted to acknowledge his own disappointments. The psychological significance of the sense of shame Hopkins felt at having failed in his vocation can be understood by referring to some studies done on the psychology of shame and self-consciousness and their social implications. Arnold H. Buss in *Self-Consciousness and*

Social Anxiety comes to the following conclusion:

> The ashamed person cannot look another person in the eye. Gaze is averted, or the face is covered with the hands. Sometimes there is a stricken look....Severe shame looks very much like depression. (149)[14]

Among literary figures, Oedipus, who suffers extreme shame, puts out his eyes as an act of atonement. Miltonic self-awareness of guilt and shame in Adam and Eve after the Fall results in avoidance of contact with eyes. They are blinded by tears of mortification later. King Lear, though not physically blinded like Gloucester, is blinded by tears when he is reconciled with Cordelia. Here, as in *Paradise Lost*, the blindness through tears of shame and mortification leads to a new vision and relief from the burden of sin. In Hopkins' "No Worst there is None" (Sonnet 65), the persona addresses the Lear-like self: "Here! creep,/wretch, under a comfort serves in a whirlwind." It was through shame and self-recognition that Lear could finally find rest and comfort in Cordelia. The desire to be thus transformed and the fear and despair that the transformation may never take place, that the "Jack, Jake, poor potsherd, patch, matchwood" of self may never turn into the "immortal diamond," underlies Hopkins' sonnets of desolation.

The failure to see, whether physical or metaphorical (because of the strictures of the ascetic life as a Jesuit, because of nervous exhaustion which dulled his sensory perceptions and because of self-attribution of personal defect resulting in shame), also implied his sense of failure as poet. The seeing/not seeing dichotomy is intrinsic to understanding the inscapes of Hopkins' poetry. The inscapes appeal to our ability to look at things with extreme care, to observe the shape and pattern of each individual being. Seeing, in Hopkins' poetry, is a dramatic act of inscaping. Often it is expressed in the persona's spontaneous interjection: "Look! Mark" ("The Wreck of the Deutschland"). This ability to see is a celebration of the inscapes of God: "To see Thee I must see Thee" ("Half-Way House"). "The Habit of Perfection" records a way of life in which the persona has failed to observe the inscapes and is, therefore, blinded with "shelled, eyes with double dark" (through an ascetic denial of the senses or a poetic phase of the exhaustion of the senses, as expressed in "A Vision of the Mermaids" and "The Escorial"). What despaired Hopkins was not that he had to sacrifice the keenness of his poetic perceptions and give up the sensuous life, for he was ready to do these, but the fact that life as a Jesuit offered him nothing but a draining of his very spirit so that while he could possibly have said, "All my eyes see," he felt the failure of the self expressed in "Carrion Comfort" as the persona's "wrestling" with God.

Frustrated by the disappointments of the priestly vocation, Hopkins returned to poetry and revived the dual-natured identity of the poet-priest self. No doubt, this meant a revival of his own sense of poetic failure as well as an affirmation of his desire to risk failure in search of perfection. In the early poems the dual persona prevails; the artist's questioning of his own creative resources and output can be traced to the aspirations set by the young visionary. Although the poem "The Alchemist in the City" cannot be read as merely allegorical, the alchemist who fails to transform lead into gold in the poem can be seen as the artistic projection of the failed miracle: loss of inspiration. John Robinson in *In Extremity: A Study of Gerard Manley Hopkins* observes:

> The Alchemist is symbolic of all who try for the magnificent and risk failing even in the ordinary. His recondite practice acts equally well as an image for artistic creation and as one for laborious scholarship. (152)[15]

In the poem, the artist's complaint is that while "the whole world passes; I stand by." One way out is escapism, a flight from the city to the wilderness. Here the alchemist contents himself by piercing the yellow glow of the sky with his eyes before he dies. There is no true transformation here; the willed act of self-banishment dissipates into a kind of mind-lulling passivity which in no way helps him deal with his feeling of artistic incapability or powerlessness.

The revived poet's movement away from escapism and towards self-confrontation is a painful one; in recording this movement, Hopkins confronts the risks and the rewards of self-exposure and self-expression. A careful reading of one of Hopkins' major poems, "The Windhover," reveals the different levels at which Hopkins confronted his own conflicts. In the beginning of the sestet, the persona defines his own role as that of an observer. He could have passively recorded his observations as the young romantic in "The Alchemist in the City" does. But, in "The Windhover," the persona's record is fused with an awareness of his own activity: "I caught this morning morning's minion." What he has caught is the inscape of the Windhover: the "riding," "rolling," "striding," "swinging," "gliding" motions of the bird coalescing to rebuff "the big wind." The poet-persona is no longer a mere observer. Awakening to the miracle of the bird's self-expression, which can create beauty in the face of self-exposure, the persona dares to do what all poets must; he expresses himself: "My heart in hiding/Stirred for a bird,—the achieve of, the mastery of the thing!" (69). This moment of awakening, however, is not like that of the Romantics, slow, dreamlike. Rather, the experience of awakening to inspiration and its effects is miraculous.

Emerging from his hiding, the persona is poised for great heights. The words at the end of the sestet, "Stirred for a bird," prepare the reader for the persona's metaphorical movement toward the bird, a creature of heights. Instead of this symbolic ascent, the reader with the persona is successively pulled down from the sky to the earth. Underlying the surface conflict of reader-expectation and dramatic development of the poem is a deeper, more fundamental concept, that of transformation. The word "transformation" is widely understood as the process of change from one state or form to another. It is a word used to describe some of the most mystical as well as some of the most physical aspects of life. In Physics, the word "transform" means "to change into another form or energy" (*Random House* 1394).[16] In "The Windhover," the first three lines of the octave illustrate the transformation of physical beauty into spiritual beauty. In this reading, Norman MacKenzie's explication of the variously interpreted word "buckle" is significant:

> The reference to the brilliant fire which results from the buckling suggests to me that Hopkins may possibly have had at the back of his mind that the buckling completed an electric circuit AND that this resulted in the production of a blinding arc of light....God's grandeur (in No. 31, 11. 1, 2) is obviously thought of as an electric charge which will flame out like lightning....In the *Sermons* (195) creatures, the "works of God's finger"—the windhover being a fine example—are said to be "charged" with the Holy Ghost, "and if we know how to touch [or "catch"] them give off sparks and take fire." (82-83)[17]

On one level, the physical beauty of the bird is transformed into its spiritual beauty. On the other level, the persona's impression of the bird's apparent mastery is modified to include an understanding of the bird's servitude to a "lovelier, more dangerous" force, Christ. The final three lines of the octave emphasize the persona's transformation of self-diffidence to self-fulfillment. True humility, not mere self-effacement, is an act of courage; it can transform "blue-bleak embers" to "gold-vermilion."

The poet-persona, in "The Windhover," is involved in defining the movement from his early escapist tendencies, through his highly sensuous and emotive self-expressions, to his creatively humble poems and self-sacrificial acts. The persona is thus mapping out the spiritual growth of his own poetic perceptions. The reader too actively participates in the creative transformation of fragmentary impressions and conflicting expectations into what Wolfgang Iser, in his theories of reader-response criticism in *The Act of Reading*, referred to as a "synthesizing activity" (119).

Hopkins had expressed the state of self-transformation in an earlier poem, "Lines from a Picture of St. Dorothea"; the poet, however, could re-capture only traces, "the rinds" and "remainder" of such a miracle (Hopkins 36). In "The Windhover," The poet shapes his language to resonate with the power, the danger and the wonder of such a transformation. Marylou Motto, in *Mined with a Motion*, records this gesture of assent to "the celebration of God in the world":

> Hopkins' unreachable ideal is one that denies the Wordsworthian process of a journey of gradual change or approach and is instead an act of heroism in man that spells total transformation and not merely assent—an apocalyptic event that would escape any located time and place and wholly transform the self. (39)[18]

At this time in his poetic career, Hopkins had himself emerged from the self-imposed artistic impotency of seven years (1868-1875); he had consciously smothered the gleams of poetic inspiration and let the magic die in the cause of a more regulated, pragmatic, and even a safer though, eventually, an artistically frustrating way of giving glory to God. On being asked by a Jesuit superior to write a poem commemorating the memory of drowned Franciscan nuns, Hopkins felt justified to come out from his hiding. The seven year period, no doubt, was fruitful in strengthening Hopkins' spiritual beliefs and training. But it was, nevertheless, a period of hiding from the wonder of artistic creation. In several poems, Hopkins captures the moment of the persona's stepping out of his hiding into the magic of self-transformation through poetic power. "The Wreck of the Deutschland" inscapes the process of emergence and the discovery of poetic inspiration as the persona's spiritual and poetic celebration of God's glory, mystery and power. The sense of freedom, of magnitude and generosity of feeling and spirit experienced on emerging from the hiding is communicated through the physical gesture of kissing his hand to the stars (Hopkins 53). In "The Windhover" the persona inscapes a similar emergence of the poetic inspiration, "My heart in hiding/Stirred for a bird," which draws the reader back to the first few words: "I *caught* this morning" (emphasis mine). Marylou Motto aptly interprets the expression as the "hand within the mind" (17). In its intense celebration of God and its creatures, the poetic inspiration is a concentration of spiritual, mental and physical energies. This magical transformation of the poet-persona is imaged in "Hurrahing in Harvest" as the heart with wings (70). The heart itself becomes the image of inspiration; this process of internalizing the source of poetic creation is a significant move in the development of Hopkins' poetry. Even as the Romantic bird of inspiration is internalized in the heart with wings, the outer landscape, the platform and subject of poetic creation, becomes internalized too:

> 0 the mind, mind has mountains, cliffs of fall
>   Frightful, sheer, no-man-fathomed. (100)

This moment of internalizing poetic inspiration is crucial in another sense too. Internalizing the source of poetic inspiration implies the greater responsibility of the artist towards creating his art. In "Poem 66," the poet-persona looks to all external sources of inspiration which have failed in one way or the other: his family, England and its indifference to his poetry, Ireland where he is only a "stranger," and prayers that go "unheard and unheeded." The poet here is still externalizing the source of his poetic inspiration and is able to lay blame elsewhere for his poetic failure. From this role of "a lonely began" ("Poem 66"), more sinned against than sinning, the persona moves to the image of self in exile as "the lost," with whom he identifies ("Poem 67"). He hurls himself into self-condemnation: "I am gall, I am heartburn," "Selfyeast of spirit, a dull dough sours" (Poem 67) and "We hear our hearts grate on themselves" (Poem 68). The poems in which the persona attempts to find a medium between the extremes of externalization or internalization are striking in their tone of quiet reconciliation to the reality of poetic endeavor, success and failure. They are also marked by a strain of painful self-awareness as the above stated poems were, but here the poet-persona encounters the creative self neither with self-praise nor with self-depreciation. In "Poem 68," the healing of the past wounds is realized by patience, a quality possessed by God, one who "distills/Delicious kindness." In Poem 69, the poet asks himself to be kinder to the creative self and avoid his own self-torment.

With patience and kindness to self comes a recognition that poetic creation is dependent on self's generosity towards itself and acceptance of its jaded "Jackself" when inspiration fails, as well as on the mercy and kindness of the Lord who can sustain the self-tormented "Time's eunuch" (here devoid of both masculine and feminine selves) with the rain of creative fertility. In all the above three poems the feminine images of vegetation and growth abound. In Poem 68, patience is described as "Natural heart's ivy"; in Poem 69, the poet asks himself to "leave comfort root-room"; in Poem 74, the poet asks the "lord of life" to "send my roots rain." The final poem, "To R.B.," treats the theme of poetic failure in a way that combines all the above approaches: the poet is pained by the loss of the "rapture of an inspiration," but he refrains from mere self-condemnation or bitter flailing at external forces.

By choosing to give expression to the two vocational aspects of the poet-priest self, Hopkins was experiencing the individuality of self at its keenest. In his notes on the *Principium sive Fundamentum*, Hopkins had elaborated on the individuality of self as a matter of pitch or taste. A look at the quotation clarifies the dual nature of the individual self (its beauty and its danger) Hopkins grapples with in his poetry. Here he expresses a kind of Romantic solipsism combined with Christian determinism: "I find myself both as man and as myself something most determined and distinctive, at pitch, more distinctive and higher pitched than anything else I see" (Devlin, ed., 121). The very individuality of self, which is the essence of its beauty, can lead to its inscrutability. The individuality of each self, that which gives it its unique identity, can also hurl it into a prison of loneliness. The impossibility to penetrate the other self's individuality catapults the self into a keener awareness of its own individuality, its own uniqueness and ultimately its own loneliness, "when I compare my self, my being myself, with anything else whatever, all things alike, all in the same degree, rebuff me with blank unlikeness" (122-123). This distinctiveness of the self, expressed as its inscape, is celebrated by Hopkins in poem after poem. In "The Wreck of the Deutschland," the nun, who rose like a lioness arose, is unique in her spiritual faith and strength, towering above the doubting and the weak. Similarly, the response of the poet-persona is one of acute physical strain, expressed as a unique individual's unique response: "Ah, touched in your bower of bone,/Are you!" It is the intense, self-reflexive language, striking in its syntax, metaphor and use of exclamations, that surprises the reader into re-living the beauty of the individual self in its act of selving. In "As Kingfishers Catch Fire," the persona relates the selving act of each individual thing to its purpose in life. The beauty of the nun, the poet, the kingfishers and others glows from this serving act. Yet, in some poems Hopkins hints at a quality of the individual self he refers to as "dangerous." In "The Windhover" the bird's beauty is surpassed by Christ's; in its uniqueness, Christ's beauty is more inscrutable, more unknowable by the senses, and therefore more "alone" than anything else in the world. This is the mystery of Christ celebrated in Catholicism, and Hopkins' poetry reiterates its impact on the individual self of the persona and the reader: "His mystery must be instressed, stressed" (Hopkins 53). It is also this quality of Christ which, while startling the priest-poet persona to deepest celebration, also plummets him down the "cliffs of fall." It is the inscrutability of Christ which appears magnified in the priest-poet's struggle; the unknowable becomes terrifying.

In the early poems the persona had asserted the dangers of physical beauty, placing spiritual beauty above it, as in Poem 16 and "The Habit of Perfection." In "The Caged Skylark," the persona attempts to understand the harmony with which the body and the spirit work. The unique inscape of physical beauty leads to, as observed, a dual response: one of joy or of fear. Paradoxically, in the "terrible sonnets" the persona emphasizes the bitterness of self-taste before realizing spiritual beauty, as in "I Wake and Feel" or the bruising impact of God's wringing foot as in "Carrion Comfort." The difference between this fleeing and the one expressed in "The Wreck of the Deutschland" is that here his fleeing from God's physical and spiritual beauty leads him to no spiritual comfort. The state resulting from this recognition is chaotic, like being tossed in a "whirlwind." The repetition of questions, of words and exclamations create the effect of an ever-recurring, circular motion, sometimes ineffectual but at other times crucial to renewed selving. David Downes, in his reading of "Carrion Comfort" comments on "the volitional energy of his renewed determination to reclaim his selfness" (*Hopkins* 19). He argues that the sonnet is not about the "terror of defeat" but about "the triumph of recovery" (19-20). Describing the sonnets as instances of Hopkins' "hermeneutic collapse" and "hermeneutic dilemmas" (17), Downes clearly articulates the movement, in some of these poems, from "spiritual hermeneutics gone awry" to the mending of the " broken hermeneutic circle" (19-20).

In the "Terrible Sonnets," the spiritual beauty of God isolates, rebuffs, mystifies and torments the poet-priest persona. Answers to his turbulent questioning are rarely forthcoming, but when they are, they affirm the mystery of the man-God relationship. "To What Serves Mortal Beauty?" was written in August 1885, about the same time as the sonnets were conceived (Gardner, Mackenzie, ed. 285). Here the persona realizes that the answer is not so much to be found in God's selfhood, but in the give and take relationship between God and man and in the acknowledgment of God's grace. In emerging from his hiding to receive God's grace, man becomes the link between the divine and the human. In *The Notebooks and Papers*, Hopkins gives the theological meaning of grace: "For grace is any action, activity on God's part by which, in creating or after creating, he carries the creature to or towards the end of its being, which is its selfsacrifice to God and its salvation" (House, ed. 332). [20] Besides receiving grace, man can be carried toward contact with God through an act of surrender. By accepting the reality of the separation between the individual human self and the individual divine self, he is able to come to a state of self-giving: "For I greet him the days I meet him, and bless when I under-/stand."

To have reached a point where a man can turn his head from the tempest and say "then leave, let that alone" ("To What Serves Mortal Beauty," 98), or even accept the fact that not all of God's mystery will ever be known or understood by man, is to have made peace with God and self, even as Hamlet with his final "surrender" does in Shakespeare's play.[21] In his tenacious probing of reality, Hamlet must act, but in order to act genuinely, to act with an absolute coherence of will, passion and reason, he knows his conscience must be in consonance with genuine emotion. This is his historical burden; he takes this burden responsibly and is reluctant to accept the roles which the ghost or his parents or the world wish to impose on him. As both player and critic, Hamlet feels all the self-divisions of the self-conscious man. He must get a coherent self to get a coherent action. He cannot be avenger and believe that his action is genuine unless the world is coherent for him. Hamlet does realize that it is impossible to make a coherent self and a coherent world out of sheer determination; what is needed is to act with some faith. So long as he has only questions, Hamlet cannot act. His release from self-torment comes when he is able to surrender himself, when he is able to let things be.

In Hopkins' poetry too, man's salvation comes through man's surrender to his faith, through his attuning himself to the larger forces that control the world. Then, he would, like St. Alphonsus Rodriguez, be prepared to fight "the war within" (Hopkins 106). In his artistic and priestly vocations Hopkins aimed at transformation of man-self into a Christ-self; so in his poetry, the persona, "this Jack, joke, poor potsherd/patch, matchwood" would "crowd career with conquest" and become "immortal diamond." Hopkins was acutely conscious of his failures, of his lapses and his "backwardglances," yet he was also painfully aware of his efforts, his unflagging attempts at self-renewal and the unique keenness of his poetic sensibility. When he wrote to Dixon that Christ was "doomed to succeed by failure," he was echoing a belief in his own self and its resources. Both as a priest and a poet, despite poor health and failures in inspiration, Hopkins possessed a quality which his poems express through images, rhythm, language and the personality of the emerging persona—the ability to rebound, to rise when close to a fall, or even to attempt to rise.

Notes

1. Part of this chapter was derived from my paper titled "Poetry as Performance: Hopkins and Reader-Response," presented at the 1996 Annual Gerard Manley Hopkins International Summer School, at Monasterevin, Ireland, June 2-7, 1996.

2. Wolfgang Iser, *The Act of Reading: A Theory of Aesthetic Response* (Baltimore: The Johns Hopkins University Press, 1978) 118-119. This work incorporates the central theoretical notions regarding text-reader interaction which appeared in his early German piece, delivered as a lecture, "Die Appellstruktur der Texte" (1970), and later rendered in English as "Indeterminacy and the Reader's Response in Prose Fiction" in J. Hillis Miller, ed., *Aspects of Narrative: Selected Papers from the English Institute* (New York and London: Columbia University Press, 1971), 1-45. Iser's theory interprets the meaning of a text as resulting from the interaction of the reader and the text, "an effect to be experienced" rather than an "object to be defined" (10).

3. David A. Downes, "A Readers' Life: Selving Through Reading Hopkins," *Saving Beauty: Further Studies in Hopkins*, eds. Michael Allsopp and David Downes (Hamden, CT: Garland, 1994) 340.

4. Gerard Manley Hopkins, *The Poems of Gerard Manley Hopkins*, 4th ed., eds. W. H. Gardner and N. H. MacKenzie (Oxford: Oxford UP, 1967) 26-27.
   Note: All subsequent quotes from Hopkins' poems refer to the above text.

5. Deuteronomy 28: 23, *The Holy Bible*, Authorized King James Version.

6. Wendell Stacey Johnson, "Sexuality and Inscape," *The Hopkins Quarterly* III (July 1976): 65.

7. Alison Sulloway, "Hopkins, Male and Female, and the 'Tender Mothering Earth'," *The Fine Delight: Centenary Essays on Gerard Manley Hopkins*, ed. Francis L. Fennell. (Chicago: Loyola UP, 1989) 33-54. This essay should be read in conjunction with Sulloway's article "Gerard Manley Hopkins and 'Women and Men' as 'Partners in the Mystery of Redemption'," *Texas Studies in Literature and Language* 31.1 (1989): 31-51, which locates her position in the controversy regarding feminist accusations of Hopkins' sexism, to be traced to Sandra Gilbert and Susan Gubar's *The Madwoman in the Attic: The Woman Writer and the Nineteenth-Century Literary Imagination* (New Haven: Yale UP, 1979). Here they refer to Hopkins' famous letter of June 1886 to Richard Watson Dixon describing "the artist's most essential quality," that is "masterly

execution," to be "a kind of male gift."

8   Sulloway, in the above mentioned article "Gerard Manley Hopkins and 'Women and Men' as 'Partners in the Mystery of Redemption," also cites Freudian interpretations by Donna Moder in "Aspects of Androgyny, Oedipal Struggle, and Religious Defence in the Poetry of Gerard Manley Hopkins," *Literature and Society* 32.1 (1986): 2-3, and the defensive responses by Jeffrey Loomis' Jungian interpretation in "Birth Pangs in Darkness: Hopkins's Archetypal Christian Biography," Texas Studies in Literature and Language 28 (1986): 81-82. Here Loomis excuses Hopkins' language by describing his imagination as androgynous. Sulloway attempts, as she claims, "a resolution between these two conflicting beliefs about Hopkins's vision of women's selves and women's worth" by clearly acknowledging his misogyny and disturbing treatment of women yet she also reveals Hopkins' maturing heroism as one that involves "modification of old self-destructive visions and the adoption of new ones" so that his "gradual reconciliation with women was a crucial sign of his hard-won maturity" (34, 48-49).

9   Claude Colleer Abbott, ed., *The Correspondence of Gerard Manley Hopkins and Richard Watson Dixon* (London: Oxford UP, 1935) 75-76.

10   Claude Colleer Abbott, ed., *Further Letters of Gerard Manley Hopkins* (London: Oxford UP, 1956) 148.

11   Claude Colleer Abbott, ed., *The Letters of Gerard Manley Hopkins to Robert Bridges* (London: Oxford UP, 1935) 190.

12   Paddy Kitchen, *Gerard Manley Hopkins* (New York: Atheneum, 1979) 145.

13   Christopher Devlin, S. J., ed., *The Sermons and Devotional Writings of Gerard Manley Hopkins* (London: Oxford UP, 1959) 61, 165.

14   Arnold H. Buss, *Self-Consciousness and Social Anxiety* (San Francisco: W. H. Freeman, 1980) 149.

15   John Robinson, *In Extremity: A Study of Gerard Manley Hopkins* (Cambridge: Cambridge UP, 1978) 152.

16   The Random House College Dictionary, rev. ed. (New York: Random House, 1980) 1394.

17 Norman MacKenzie, *A Reader's Guide to Gerard Manley Hopkins* (Ithaca: Cornell University Press, 1981) 82-83.

18 Marylou Motto, *Mined With a Motion: The Poetry of Gerard Manley Hopkins* (New Jersey: Rutgers University Press, 1984) 39.

19 David Anthony Downes, *Hopkins' Achieved Self* (Lanham, Maryland: University Press of America, 1996) 19, 20.

20 Humphrey House, ed., *The Notebooks and Papers of Gerard Manley Hopkins* (London: Oxford UP, 1937) 332.

21 William Shakespeare, *William Shakespeare: The Complete Works*, ed. Alfred Harbage (New York: The Viking Press, 1969) 971.

Chapter 2

The Self and the Other: Response to Failure in Communication

The conditions of isolation and association experienced by the poet-priest persona in Hopkins' poems are reiterated not only in the thematic concerns but also in the rhetorical structure of the persona-reader-subject relationship. The first half of this chapter will deal with the thematic variations of the relationship between the self and the other and the latter half with the rhetorical structure of the poems emphasizing the artistic concern with "the other," the reader. Hopkins' response to breaks in communication between the priest-self and the parish community, between the poet-self and the reader-subject entity are relevant in understanding the evolving role of self in the face of failure.

One of the major tensions in Hopkins' poetry, that of human isolation and human association, was not only the outcome of his chosen careers of priest and poet; each of the chosen spheres embodied a duality of roles and functions. St. Ignatius Loyola's *Spiritual Exercises* emphasized the need for meditation and spiritual seclusion, as is evident in the twentieth annotation of the guidelines provided for the retreatant and the director:

> In these he will, ordinarily, more benefit himself, the more he separates himself from all friends and acquaintances and from all earthly care, as by changing from the house where he was dwelling, and taking another house or room to live in, in as much privacy as he can, so that it be in his power to go each day to Mass and to Vespers, without fear that his acquaintances will put obstacles in his way.[1]

On the other hand, the duties of the priest involved taking care of his parish in human terms; it meant looking after the sick, the poor, blessing those who came for communion and praying for those who did not. As a priest, Hopkins' main duties were teaching, which meant associating and communicating with students. As a poet too, Hopkins felt the dual pull toward isolation and association. In his early poetry, Hopkins withdrew from the community to dwell on his closeness to nature and to inscape his individuality. His isolation heightened his sense of loneliness, the central experience of the Romantics. On the other hand, as a poet writing in the Victorian milieu, Hopkins could never be blind to the social connection of man. The difference between the two chosen careers rested upon how successful Hopkins was in resolving the conflicts of isolation and association. As a priest, Hopkins openly expressed his own frustrations. As a poet, he found an imaginative outlet. Hopkins' poetry is the ground where the priest and the poet's sense of isolation and of communion find expression in the evolving sensibility of the persona. In some poems, the sense of despair and "encagement," as Donald Walhout puts it, is overpowering.[2] In others, Hopkins' persona achieves a communion with a fellow sufferer or even a stranger, so that in those instances "world sorrow" is transformed by association with "World's loveliest—men's selves."[3]

Bell Gale Chevigny in "Instress and Devotion in the Poetry of Gerard Manley Hopkins" outlines the three phases of Hopkins' mature poetry: the early period of inscapes in the "natural world," the middle period of inscapes in "the human beings with whom Hopkins has to deal as a priest," and the late period of inscapes in "versions of his own soul" (145).[4] However, Chevigny, in his analysis, assumes that the experiences of isolation and association in Hopkins' poetry were chronological or linear in time. William B. Thesing, on the other hand, more realistically notes recurring instances of poems dealing with human isolation and association:

> In all of Hopkins' poems about people, from the 1879-80 group of "Henry Purcell," "Felix Randal," and "Cheery Beggar" to the 1887 group of "Harry Ploughman" and "Tom's Garland" and the 1888-89 group of "In Honour of St. Alphonsus Rodriguez" and "The Shepherd's Brow," the poet struggles to order and harmonize difficulties that he sees in the figures' lives (37).[5]

The variations in these groups emphasize the nature of Hopkins' faith which was "intensely optimistic" in the early years, but became chaotic and pessimistic in the 1887 period, finally to re-affirm the inscapes of humanity again in the 1888-89 group.

The attempt in this chapter is to understand some of the factors underlying the isolation of Hopkins' persona from human figures and the implications of his attempts at re-integration with them within the framework of the poem. The poems of isolation from humanity deal, in most part, with three kinds of isolation: isolation from family (paralleling Hopkins' isolation from family due to religious conversion), isolation from homeland (the priestly duties "banished" him to work in Wales and in Ireland; moreover, his poetry was rejected in his own country, England), and isolation from humanity in general (which springs from four main factors: the fallen condition of man, the extreme sense of failure in self, the modern man's experience of existential loneliness and Hopkins' romanticism). The poems of association deal with all these four factors and emphasize the possibility of man's renewal through human association.

In "To Seem the Stranger Lies My Lot, My Life" (101), written probably in 1885, the persona expresses the gulf between his Anglican family and himself due to his conversion to Catholicism. His isolation from his homeland is of two kinds: he is in Ireland "among strangers," which makes him an exile. In life, continual rejection of Hopkins' poetry by publishers in England due to "his development of a strange and difficult poetic style and rhythm" frustrated him and left his works "unheard" and "unheeded" (MacKenzie 179).[6] The sense of isolation is captured by the persona in the striking description of himself as "a lonely began." The noun-equivalent "began" does not carry the promise of the fulfilment of the execution implied in "beginner." It emphasizes, as James Finn Cotter observes the implications of the use of interjections in the poem to imply, "the cry of distress" expressed by the persona "as truth hits home" (288-89).[7]

Hopkins' alienation from England, mainly because of his religious conversion to Catholicism, and his need and impulse to be accepted and recognized by his countrymen translates into split images of the "exiled persona" that observes and critiques conditions in England, and the "patriotic persona" who evokes the jingoism of late nineteenth century imperial Britain. In a poem like "What Shall I do for the Land that Bred Me," the voice of the patriotic persona rings with epic heroic quality as he enumerates the rhetorical phases of a "true" soldier's commitment to his country: "I'll live for her honour," "and fight for honour" and finally "I fall for her honour," where death becomes a martyr's sacrifice: "Immortal beauty is death with duty" (195). However, counter to this rhetorical optimism runs the exiled persona's bleaker view of England. At first, his criticism is subtle, often generalized as the desire to escape spatial and geographical boundaries to utopian lands: "I have desired to go/where springs not fail" ("Heaven-Haven," 19). His later criticism of industrialized England is evident even in the early poems' persona as he rejects the city for the country: "No, I should love the city less/...But I desire the wilderness" ("The Alchemist in the City," 25). England's Protestantism is also rejected as the persona forsakes his "national and Egyptian reed" ("Half-way House," 28), explained by Gardner and MacKenzie as forsaking the "'national' religion of the Established Church (that) had failed to satisfy G. M. H." ("Notes" 251). Later the persona as "exiled nun" in "The Wreck of the Deutschland" becomes the prophetess who through her martyred death will "intercede for the conversion of 'rare-dear Britain'" ("Notes" 255).

The two opposing personae assess their attitudes towards England in terms of specific locales and time frames. Among the places in England that the patriotic personae evoke with nostalgic fondness is the "Towery City" of Oxford. The city where Duns Scotus had once lectured in 1301 ("Notes" 272), is remembered mainly for its associations with the past philosopher closest to Hopkins' spirit ("Duns Scotus' Oxford," 79). The persona refers to it as "my park, my pleasaunce," endearing both as a place of intellectual and spiritual haven, with its "quiet-walled grove" ("To Oxford," 21) and for "sweeter-memoried" associations of his past days and friends ("To Oxford," 162). In contrast to the past Oxford, present Oxford is a place where the natural environment, "the rural scene" is being "hewed" and "hacked" ("Binsey Poplars," 78). The exiled persona reappears as the alienated individual who experiences the painful historical reality of capitalistic pursuit and labor oppression. He exposes industrial England breaking "big-boned and hardy-handsome" men like Felix Randal, who as a blacksmith has suffered the fatal consequences of working in the unhealthy environment of industrial pollution in places like Manchester and Liverpool. The alienated persona finds little religious consolation or even human dignity in the poverty and oppressive conditions of the laboring class. Unlike the Cheery Beggar "whom want could not make pine" (179), the day laborer in "Tom's Garland" is at his "low lot"; as the unemployed, he has become "prick proof," beyond feeling hunger and sickness (103).

Hopkins never did attempt to intellectually resolve these opposing strains that run through his poems. However, he did create personae who avoid extremes of patriotic jingoism and bleak pessimism. In these personae's voices bombast and rhetoric is displaced by religious symbolism; the alienated individual is transformed into the inhabitant of an integrated community. Unlike the trite, patriotic song "What Shall I do for the Land that Bred Me," "The Soldier" is a "homeland" poem of human bonding and association. It reveals the misleading criteria of manliness based on appearances, adopted by the general mass. Hopkins' persona pitches Christ's true service as against the people's sentimental opinion of the "soldier." The persona at first includes himself with the unseeing "seeing" mass, blessing the "redcoats" and "tars." This identification of himself with the masses is a clear indication of his fallible humanness and his humility. It becomes the platform from which he can instress Christ as king and soldier, fighting the higher war.

The isolation from humanity in general was triggered by at least four main factors as mentioned above. In the inscapes of human figures, Hopkins' persona faces and attempts to resolve the despair caused by the sense of original sin and, hence, the ultimate damnation of man. In "Spring and Fall," the persona solves the mystery of Margaret's mourning; she is mourning for the blight of man, for the universal condition of man, expressed as the "woe" and the "world sorrow" in the Terrible Sonnet 65, "No Worst, There is None." How can man leave his mark in these conditions? One answer lies in the inscapes of the "World's loveliest—men's selves" (98). W. H. Gardner in his study of Hopkins had noted that "inscape" for Hopkins implied "the hand of God upon his Creation," and that "the perception of inscape in Hopkins is marked simultaneously, as a rule, by the flow of instress, as though the individual beholder becomes mystically one with the whole, and seems to imply a supernatural force which binds in, bounds the infinite one" (11-12).[8] Moreover, John Wain points out, in "An Idiom of Desperation," that in Gardner's definition, "instress is not only the unifying force *in* the object; it connotes also the impulse from the 'inscape' which acts *on* the stress and through them, actualizes the inscape in the mind of the beholder (or rather 'perceiver,' for inscape may be perceived through all the senses at once)" (64-65).[9] Thus the moments of inscape and instress are the moments of fusion of being and thought; in the inscapes of human figures, the perceiver and the perceived join in the experience of oneness, reaching its highest pitch in the realization of "the hand of God upon His Creation." This experience can be extended to the evolving relationship of the reader and the persona. Even as the persona is the perceiver of his world, the Hopkins' reader participates as the perceiver of the persona and his interactions with nature, man, God and self. In a way, the effect of Hopkins' poem on the reader is one of a reiterated instress—one through imaginative empathy with the persona and one through the immediacy of responses to the persona's act of instressing. Thus the reader fulfills within the reader-self the persona's celebration of the individual inscape.

Hopkins' persona, besides associating with the sick and the poor, feels an affinity with the figures of the past. In "Duns Scotus's Oxford," the persona revisiting Oxford evokes the golden period of the middle ages. The city as he sees it now has lost its unifying way of life. Yet the figure who best embodied the true mark, Duns Scotus, has left his imprint in the very air the persona gathers and releases. In inscaping Duns Scotus, the persona is reviving those distinctive qualities in human figures which become expressions of the ultimate beauty of God. Henry Purcell, the seventeenth century musician, is another such figure inscaped by the persona, in the poem "Henry Purcell." In the Preface to the poem, Hopkins praises him for having expressed his individual mark, as well as inscapes of all humans, in his music (80). The sonnet's moment of inscape is clearly marked in comparing Purcell to a stormfowl whose "colossal/smile" awakens a sense of wonder in the viewer. In his letter to Robert Bridges, Hopkins explained that he valued Purcell for his unique individuality (170).[10]

But what does the poem as the expression of a persona's experience convey to the reader, what emotions does it evoke and how? These are questions which can be answered by observing the reader's responses to the expression of the persona-self. The persona's first line strikes one as an ambiguous combination of two states of the perceiving self—the questioning, doubting, hesitant state, beginning with the self's interrogative "Have fair fallen," only to merge into the state of realization charged with emotional intensity: "O fair, fair have fallen." A sense of the persona's passivity and activity in the expression of Purcell's inscape is developed in the poem in terms of being acted upon or acting (80). The movement from the initial "me" and "I" as the perceiver to the final "our" involves the growing identity of the reader with the persona. It is through the experience of inscape and instress that the relationship between the persona and the reader reaches a point of shared wonder.

The poem "In Honour of St. Alphonsus Rodriguez" (1888) is about one of the lay brothers of Hopkins' order, St. Alphonsus Rodriguez (1533-1617), who had been a watchman and porter for forty years at the Jesuit College at Montesion in Palma, Majorca. The poem, though an occasional piece, is sincere in its celebration of a hero who struggled against the inner war, the various temptations by which God tested him. Through his patience, duty and purity of mind, he identified himself with

Christ, who is inscaped by the persona as one who can "crowd career with conquest" (106). It is in the moments of inscape and instress that the poet can establish a bond with the figures who are dead and gone, even as in the parenthetical asides he establishes a communicative bond with the reader. These poems are, in a way, answers to the regret expressed in "The Lantern Out of Doors," "No worst, There is None," and "That Nature is a Heraclitean Fire"—that distance and death end all individuals (71, 100, 105).

In "The Handsome Heart" (1879), the moment of human association is the moment of the priest-persona's perception of the beauty of character in the young boy who served with no desire for rewards. By expressing itself instinctively, the being, which is "Mannerly-hearted! more than handsome face," chooses the right course. In "The Bugler's First Communion" (1879), the moment of sacramental interaction between the priest-persona and the bugler, and finally between the bugler and God, is expressed in an image of the youth's coming of age compared to a ripening peach (83). But there is another relationship that is partially developed throughout the poem—the relationship between the persona and the reader. The reader anticipated here is an outsider; in the very first line the persona explains parenthetically the location of the barracks from where the Bugler boy came. At this point, the persona's communication with the reader is based mainly on revealing facts and carefully substantiating the source of his information, and expressing his personal views in parenthesis. From addressing the reader mainly in asides, the persona shifts to address the "divine" "heavens," though the complicated syntax in lines thirteen and fourteen is baffling to the reader. Norman MacKenzie unravels some of the complication when he points out, "In stanza four, 'ah divine' is marooned from its original noun, as we realize from the first fragmentary draft: 'Your sweetest sendings, ah divine/Heavens befall him!'" (MacKenzie 125). From addressing the "divine" "heavens" and the "angel-warder," the persona returns to identify the reader with his community by using pronouns "us" and "our" (lines 30 and 40). But the reader-involvement is scattered by the constant shifts in the persona's choice of addressee. Another effect, noted by MacKenzie, is deliberate reversal of the reader's expectations which has the effect of startling him/her rather than establishing a rapport: "He deliberately reverses our expectations: in defiance of normal usage he calls lads who are true to their own noble inscape of gracious personality 'headstrong' (st. 6); instead of putting a 'ban on' someone (a curse or anathema), the sealing chrism 'bans off' evil (st. 9). So too the 'divine doom' in stanza eleven is, surprisingly, a favouring providence." (125)

Norman MacKenzie's comment on Hopkins' sense of failure in poetic quality is also significant; it accounts for the constant shifts in reader-involvement:

> His lament that he has nothing to show for his labours reflects both the loneliness of the artist, and a personal feeling of being a misfit among the crowds. He ends with a Romantic yearning to escape to the solitude of the wilderness, no matter how bleak. (24)

The desire for "the houseless shore" and "the wilderness" implies the persona's separation from the city and the crowds, often paralleled, in Hopkins' poems, by the distancing of the persona from the reader. The communion the persona wishes to establish is with nature. This Romantic tendency is manifest in Hopkins' early poetry, and is a kind of prison to which, as J. Hillis Miller notes, "Paterian phenomenalism had condemned him" (224).[11] Later, he subordinated the sensuous beauty of the world to God's spiritual grace. Yet, through inscaping God in natural beauty, Hopkins' poetry is a romantic response to the existential dilemma of the twentieth century. In J. Hillis Miller's view there have been a number of responses to the disappearance of God:

> But a group of Victorian poets belong to another tradition: romanticism. The romantics still believe in God, and they find his absence intolerable. At all cost they must attempt to re-establish communication. Romanticism defines the artist as the

> creator or discoverer of new symbols, symbols which establish a new relation, across the gap, between man and god....The central assumption of romanticism is the idea that the isolated individual, through poetry, can accomplish the "unheard of work," that is, create through his own efforts a marvelous harmony of words which will reintegrate man, nature and God. (211-212)

Hopkins' God is, on the one hand, an external power, particularized by his finer or higher pitch.[12] On the other hand, he is "the most complex pattern of all" who "contains in himself the archetypes of all things" (Miller 225). The contradiction about the self evolving from the "contradiction about the nature of God" is, as J. Hillis Miller suggests, "at the heart of the poet's spiritual experience": individuality is both "a matter of pitch, of taste, something so highly tuned and idiosyncratic that it is like nothing else in the world," and also "a matter of complexity and fineness of pattern," containing in himself "all the creatures lower than he in the scale of being" (225-26).

This brings us to the poems in which Hopkins expresses "resonances" between the persona and other men. These moments become the moments of the renewal of self from the personal despair of failure as well as from the "ultima solitude" in Scotus' phrase. These poems deal with the persona's inscapes of the sick or victims of society, and of the poor and the working men. "Felix Randal," one of the best of these humanistic poems, was written at the Liverpool city slums on 28 April 1880 (MacKenzie 135). The news of the blacksmith's death leads the priest-persona to a rehearsal of the sickness that "broke him." The empathy between the priest and Felix, that resulted out of the suffering of and compassion for the blacksmith, is captured in a tender moment. In a structural analysis of line nine, "My tongue had taught thee comfort, touch had quenched thy/tears," Joseph Eble notes the inversion of phrase and sound in the second half of the line as being significant in conveying the nature of the "sacramental consolation":

> The reader is swept into a dynamic movement of sound and meaning that seems, in

three closely linked structures, to take him forward and then backward. There is, it would seem, a mimetic struggle for contact between the speaking poet and the figure of the blacksmith. The two-way syntax suggests a two-way relationship. Through the exchange of love, poet and blacksmith are brought together and almost merge. The relationship clearly becomes much more than the mere "duty" it is at first labeled. (131-32).[13]

The moment of inscaping and instressing the beauty of the farrier's body and character is a coalescence of the two-way relationship in Hopkins' unique poetic vision.

While "Cheery Beggar" (dated probably 1879), among "the unfinished poems, fragments and light verse," is a simple poem of a carefree, undespairing beggar who has not been seared by his "struggling," "Tom's Garland" (written in 1887) is a gloomy, often harsh, vision of the unemployed in Victorian England. Many critics have noted political themes in the poem. John Sutherland notes, "'Tom's Garland' is Hopkins' solitary political poem," and goes on to claim that Shakespeare's *Coriolanus* is interfused in the underthought of the poem, in that the play is "angry in tone and conservative in attitude" (115).[14] Although beginning with a traditional belief in the divine order and hierarchy of society, the tone of the persona shifts to one of sharp indignation at the animalistic state of man:

> This, by Despair, bred Hangdog dull; by Rage,
> Manwolf, worse; and their packs infest the age.
> (103)

Although Hopkins' famous 1871 letter to Bridges was surprisingly considered shocking in its controversial statement, "Horrible to say, in a manner I am a Communist," it would be reductive to consider "Tom's Garland" as a poem with a communist underthought. In one of the letters written after the "Red Letter," Hopkins contradicts his early statement and denies any sympathy for the red communes (Abbott, ed. 27, 29). Hopkins' belief in the hard work of the labourers and the working class is not so much the outcome of his political beliefs as much as of his spiritual convictions. The life of a Jesuit priest was imbued with an affirmation of the work ethic, derived directly from the teachings of St. Ignatius Loyola. In the *Notebooks*, Hopkins refers to the work ethic of all citizens of the commonwealth as "DOING THEIR DUTY" in realizing the "COMMON GOOD" (House, ed. 271-72). In *Gerard Manley Hopkins: A Very Private Life*, Robert Bernard Martin traces a link between Hopkins' poetic creation of the working man, Felix, and a passage in the *Ecclesiasticus* describing an ideal workman:

> "The smith at his anvil is absorbed in his handiwork. The breath of the fire melts his flesh and he wastes away in the heat of the furnace. He batters his ear with the din of the hammer...". Both in literal detail and suggested symbolic meaning, there is great likeness between the passage and the man. Whatever more personal feelings Hopkins may have had for the farrier..., he subdues them all to the relationship of spiritual father and child, then to the apotheosis of man and manhood at the conclusion of the poem, suggesting the natural nobility of the "workman's part in the commonweal." (329)[15]

In the poem "Tom's Garland," the persona's awareness that the unemployed had no place in the "Commonweal" leads to a tone of explosive harshness which fails to be reintegrated in a more unifying inscape. William B. Thesing comments: "The shock of explosion of the structure of feeling at the end of 'Tom's Garland' was so profound that Hopkins attempted no further inscapes of Victorian society" (47). It is a poem which hangs in the air. In his attempts to renew the self through human association, Hopkins' persona finds himself in a system which fosters bleak animality, and his response is one of frustration and chaos.

"Harry Ploughman," written in the same year as "Tom's Garland," inscapes Harry's physical beauty. Thesing points out the tortuous, complex syntax as another instance of a chaos which finds no resolution in "Tom's Garland" (41). MacKenzie notes the source of obscurity in the poem as the "deployment of words at whose meaning one can still only guess"—words like "flue," "broth," "brough," and others (193). C. Day Lewis comments: "If Harry is a monumental figure, then I get only a fly's eye view of it, a series of blinding close-ups, as if I were crawling laboriously from limb to limb over the surface of a corrugated, undemonstrative statue" (126).[16] The main flaw in the poem, according to the critics, is the failure to integrate Harry's physical beauty with a total "beauty of character." However, a close reading of the poem shows that here as in "The Caged Skylark" Hopkins reiterated the belief that "Man's spirit will be flesh-bound when found at best." The concentration on Harry's physicality has often been interpreted as Hopkins' unnatural attraction to the male figure. The act of inscaping Harry, in such a case, would be motivated by repressed sexual tension; yet one finds the description of the muscles, the ribs, the flank and other physical features, detailed, detached and scientific rather than repressed or sublimated. One of the qualities of Hopkins' persona, scientific observation infused with the vitality and abundance of emotional response, is obvious in this poem. The first eleven lines are devoted to the persona's minute observation. Then comes his emotional response, keen, wondering, connotative, urging the imagined reader to look, see, notice and witness the wonder of Harry's physical beauty. He expresses himself in imperatives and dramatic interjections, heightening the emotional response. Besides the fact that "Harry Ploughman" displays Hopkins' typical concerns in poetry at the height of poetic energies, the poem offers something else. The persona's concern with Harry's physical being leads to an expression that stands out in the poem: "He leans to it, Harry bends, look. Back, elbow, and liquid/waist." James Finn Cotter's study of Hopkins' inscapes reveals the mythopoeic ordering of the poem: "Locked to the plow, Harry Ploughman's hard as hurdle arms fuse in one sinew service' and, like the blacksmith 'at the random grim forge,' define the contour of life's destination" (282). Here Harry's bowed figure, expressing the arc of tension, is seen as the figure of the Omega, which is "the parabola and focal point of inscape, inclosed in the conic universe and heart" (277). The act of bending or leaning is also a significant two-way response of the body to the conditions of its existence—the physical condition (the body bending to work and labour) and the spiritual condition (the body rising from the fallen state to Christ, almost "wind lifted," even as the curls are). The persona's inscaping of this physical stance is a recurrent motif in Hopkins' poetry. "Easter Communion" ends with the persona's fervent prayer and hope to rise from the "bent" state. In "The Wreck of the Deutschland," the self hiding from God feels the stress of Christ and its response is one of physical leaning: "And the midriff astrain with leaning of, laced/with fire of stress" (52). In "God's Grandeur," the "bent" world is a metonymic expression of the "bent man" (bent through the "original fall" or "universal sin"). Here there is hope for the "bent World," protected by the wings of the Holy Ghost. In "The Leaden Echo and the Golden Echo," the word "back" conveys "the feeling of physical strain" (Abbott, ed. 162). In "Ribblesdale," the persona ironically stresses the fallen condition of man in physical terms: "To his own selfbent so bound, so tied to his turn" (91). In "Harry Ploughman" the motif of the bent body, especially coming after a series of descriptions that highlight the perfection of the body, reaches its climax. In one sense, bending may signify the motion from an upright state to that of the fallen. In "Ribblesdale" man's condition *is* hopeless and the "bent" state will only lead to a fall. But in another sense, "bending" may signify the motion from a fallen to an upright state. In "Harry Ploughman" the hope that is expressed in "Easter Communion," "The Wreck of the Deutschland," and "God's Grandeur" is revived. Harry, perfect in beauty like Adam in Edenic state, lives at the brink of a dangerous state—the fallen state. However, his spiritual beauty is sparked off from his action, that is bending (taking the burden of human sin and suffering, associating oneself to one's work and also preparing oneself for the spiritual heights) to transform the self into a risen state. The persona here is inscaping Harry at the moment of self-transformation through self-effort. The repetition of the "l" and "w" sounds in the latter half of the poem (as against the "b," "r," "k," "st," and "f" sounds in the first half of the poem) conveys to the reader a sense of

Harry's beauty as touched by tenderness, grace, and harmony ("liquid waist," "quail to the wallowing o' the plough") and, ultimately, "beauty of character."

In the final analysis, the poems in which Hopkins' persona inscapes human figures are significant in that they record the moments of self's association with the other and also the moments of recovery from the self's spiritual and artistic loneliness as well as solipsistic individualism. As shown in the study, the interaction of the two selves is expressed most intensely in the moment of inscape and instress. Much has been said about Hopkins' inscapes of nature; though less abundant, the inscapes of human figures in Hopkins' poems are not mere theoretical attempts at phrasing social or political ideologies. Those which attempt to grapple with some of these ideologies, as "Tom's Garland," end in unresolved chaos and frustration. On the other hand, the persona's inscapes of humanity, like the inscapes of nature, are spontaneous and intensely felt experiences of the individuality and unity of beings and are often communicated as such to the reader. In the chapter titled "Maturation," in *Send My Roots Rain,* Donald Walhout perceptively analyzes the "incarnational element" in Hopkins' "view of human association and its potentiality":

> According to that doctrine (of incarnation), the vehicle for mediation between God and man is, after all, human embodiment. Using the idea of analogy (though not referring to theological salvation), one could then say that, pristinely, all persons are potentially mediating vehicles for the restoration of other persons within the times, places and situations in which they find themselves. Just as Christ restores, each person can be a healing vehicle for another in time of trouble. In this way is the human community designed. (65)

In "As Kingfishers Catch Fire," the highly individual persona affirms the presence of Christ in other selves, even as he celebrates their individuality (90). As expressed in one of his hymns (unfinished draft, probably dated 1885), "Thee God, I Come from, to Thee, go," Hopkins' persona projects a keen awareness of the therapeutic and spiritual effects of human association; each one is the "mate and counterpart for the other" (194).

ii

As Hopkins examines the dubious qualities of the self, the other and the God-self, he relates each in a one-to-one linear strain of push and pull till it bends to a curve. It is the intensity and the tensility of the relationships that Hopkins translates into a language of kinesis. Besides the confrontation with the communal other, the poet of the poet-priest self takes into account the reader and his role. Hopkins had created another self, that of the reader, which would read, examine, penetrate, judge and finally accept or reject his work. In his letters to Bridges, Hopkins often referred to the problem of the common reader. In response to Bridges' criticism of his use of rhythm, Hopkins urged him to "hear" rather than "read" his verse, clearly stating that his poetry was not for the "public" (Abbott, ed. 46). Hopkins' notes, written on the poems sent to his own learned friends who could not understand his poetry, imply his awareness that his poems were written to selected readers—Hopkins' version of what Wolfgang Iser would call "the ideal reader," who, "unlike the contemporary reader, is a purely fictional being; he has no basis in reality, and it is this very fact that makes him so useful: as a fictional being, he can close the gaps that constantly appear in any analysis of literary effects and responses" (29). A great deal of Hopkins' poetry is dramatic precisely because it is addressing a selected group of individuals, ideal but also having its own personality, characteristics, or what Hopkins would call "Pitch" or "inscape" of self. The role of the reader in Hopkins' poetry often shifts from that of the observer to that of the addressee. In stanza three of "The Wreck of the Deutschland," as an observer, the reader is either a witness to the direct interaction of God and poet (stanzas one and twenty nine of "The Wreck") or a privileged though unacknowledged confidante, overhearing the soliloquies of the poet-priest (stanzas four and five of "The Wreck"). In stanza six of the poem, a hint that the persona is aware of the reader begins to dawn. The parenthetical aside, "(and few know this)," could imply that the reader is one of the "few." This suggestion is made obvious in stanzas eight and nine, where the persona and the reader share the experience, expressed in words like "we," "us," and "our," and respond in similar ways. So far there has been a slow evolution of the persona-reader relationship. It is in stanza twelve that a shift occurs. Stanza twelve was originally stanza one in the first drafts; however, it works better dramatically in the present position. It is in this stanza that the addressee is, for the first time, two different selves. The first four lines are the opening of the persona's narrative and are therefore addressed to the reader. The details about the time and the place of the incident and the number of the wrecked specify the reader as a person interested in facts and figures. An abrupt change has taken place in the persona's attitude to the reader. After establishing a closeness with the reader which verges on highly emotive levels of experience (notice the metaphorical language of the last four lines of stanza eleven), the persona withdraws. The reader is placed at a distance and is given prosaic details. The role of the persona veers to that of the informer, a role much easier to assume than that of the self-tormented sharer of false dreams. The withdrawal of the persona from the reader is completed in the last four lines of the same stanza. From the addressee, the reader shifts to the role of the witness. The questions buffetted by the persona to the Father are intense, soul-searing but also a mixture of appeal and reprimand. The transposed syntax "Yet did not the dark side" to "Yet did the dark side...not vault them" (55) and the positioning of the "even" (which "suggests that something mentioned as a possibility constitutes an extreme case or an unlikely instance")[17], while placing him as a bumbling expostulator, wins the reader's sympathy. Removed to the position of an observer, the reader's self understands, or is at least drawn to understand the persona speaking as an exile, bewildered by the turn of events. It is the persona who makes the reader's self act by volition, for it is at this moment of complete withdrawal that the persona is most keenly comprehensible to the reader. The hint that the persona and the reader share something, perhaps a way of experiencing intense moments, is confirmed now. The shift in the middle of stanza twelve is thus both an unpremeditated, psychologically viable, self-protective strategy of the persona and also an artist's final freeing of the reader to achieve rapport of thought, feeling and sympathy. It occurs again and again as in stanzas eighteen, twenty one (narrative and address to God), twenty five to twenty eight, and thirty one (soliloquies). In stanza thirty one, the persona shifts from addressing God to soliloquizing to addressing God again. The reader is nowhere mentioned or acknowledged. However, the paeonic sprung rhythm and the long, breathless lines draw the reader into the poem's spectrum of feeling. It is this reader-participation, worked out in the language and rhetorical substance of Hopkins' poetry, that makes the persona so accessible, often endearing.

In "The Starlight Night," the reader is urged to participate by the ecstatic, child-like exclamations of the persona. The particulars from fairy tales' lore—"the fire-folk," "the bright boroughs," "the circle-citadels," "the diamond delves," "the elves'-eyes," "quickgold," "wind-beat whitebeam!," "airy abeles," "flake-doves"—appeal to the child in the reader and he/she accordingly takes on the role of an imaginative, wide-eyed believer in miracles. After luring the reader into the child-role, the persona suddenly shifts his tone. He addresses the reader with a matter of fact, "Ah well! it is all a purchase, all is a prize./ Buy then! bid then!" (66-67). The reader must feel the abrupt change in the relationship. After the close rapport felt among children sharing the wonder and the magic of the fairy-tale world, the reader is jerked into the position of a prosaic, wordly merchant ready for a quick bargain. The relationship between the persona and the reader is one of wary businessmen at an auction, vying with each other, mature and professional, but also underlined with a camaraderie. Both know that anyone can win the prize: "Ah well! it is all a purchase, all is a prize." Having moved away from a childlike wonder to a businesslike caution, reflected in shifts in word choices, tonal effects and dramatic scenes, the persona defines his own evolving relationship to God.

He is at first struck by the beauty of God's self (inscaped in the stars and skies), but then moves to acknowledge another aspect of God's self—its inscrutability, mystery and remoteness from the poet-priest self. What he must pay in return for the miracle are "Prayer, patience, alms, vows"—duties of a Jesuit priest and also of a poet who must labor and expect no fame, who must give his wealth (poetry) to the world and make his own vows of artistic effort in the praise of God.

The poet-priest persona, by creating a reader whose role shifts in the poem, is establishing a double relationship: the poet-reader and the priest-God relationship. Through the medium of a more accessible other-self (the reader), the persona succeeds in building a rapport with Christ. After taking the cautious strategies necessary to overcome the distance between two highly developed individual selves of the persona and Christ, the persona again evokes the childlike wonder at the beauty of Christ. The miracle of "a Mayness" or a "March bloom" is more accessible than that of "fire-folk sitting in the air" or of "the circle citadels," and yet retains its magical wonder, even as the merchant's cautious camaraderie is more tractable than the dream world of children. In such ways does the persona move from the sheer wonder at Christ's remote beauty to a closer understanding of both the beauty and danger of Christ's selfhood. Affirming the priestly duties, the poet-priest is able to penetrate constructively the remoteness that separates Christ from himself. While in "To What Serves Mortal Beauty" God's "grace" saved him, and in "The Wreck of the Deutschland," he acknowledged that God's mystery is never fully knowable, in this poem the persona is ready to take the risk, to give all in order to bring Christ home (to his own heart). By working out this resolution and by their very interactions, the poet-priest persona and the reader participate in overcoming individual failures in communication and anticipate the final communion of self with God.

In "Felix Randal" the persona addresses the reader, seeking confirmation from him regarding Felix's death: "O is he dead then? (86). The reader is perhaps somebody who was close to the farrier, perhaps a relative, a friend or a coworker, in whose company the priest-persona can drift into past memories without embarrassment (lines five to eight). The persona's consoling sigh ("Ah well") and easy use of dialect ("Ah well, God rest him all road ever he offended," imply the persona's closeness to the reader-listener self, but on a well-observed priest-parish level. Even the generalization that the sight of the sick wins our sympathy is marked by the formality of a priestly duty involving consoling the bereaved and edifying the dead. So far, so good. Then, suddenly, the tone changes and so does the addressee. The poet-priest persona directly talks to Felix in a highly emotive language. The mutual give and take of human interaction is paralleled in the structure of the lines; the intensity of feeling, now no longer hidden under formal generalization, breaks out with the repetition of Felix's name: "child, Felix, poor Felix Randal." The slow sinking into past memories (sestet) is not a duty-bound attempt at consolation (for here the persona is momentarily unaware of the reader's presence), but a true expression of instress felt by him. The sincerity of feeling is communicated to the reader most intensely in these moments of the persona's withdrawal from him, even as seen in "The Wreck of the Deutschland." The intensity in the sestet works precisely because the reader has been drawn in, at first non-commitally, but later by volition. The reader, though acting by volition, has been brought to a position where he cannot but be a participant. Conceding to grant the reader artistic freedom, the poet-persona succeeds in keeping him within the parameters of his own rhetorical control.

    The poems which record the failures in communication between the priest-self and the parish-communal-self or even the God-self, that is, the Terrible Sonnets, also display a marked lack of communication between the persona and the reader; often even the attempt is not made. The despair at the distance between the two selves is reflected in the increasing solipsism of the sonnets. From the very first lines, "No worst, there is none," "I wake and feel the fell of dark," "My own heart let me more have pity on," Hopkins reveals preoccupation with the self, referred to as a pitiful "wretch" or "heart." These poems dwell on a particular kind of loss—loss of comfort felt keenly through the absence of a dear, loved one. The persona's awareness of the absence of his Paraclete, Christ or Comforter, is poetically transmitted through his conscious awareness of the reader's absence. The poet-priest self is thus completely alone. In his spiritual notes "First Principle and Foundation," Hopkins had referred to the nature of the self:

> A self then will consist of a center *and* a surrounding area or circumstance, of a point of reference *and* a belonging field, the latter set out, as surveyors etc. say, from the former; of two elements, which we may call the inset and the outsetting or the display. (House, ed. 127)

In the Terrible Sonnets, the persona's pain and despair arise out of a realization similar to that expressed by Hopkins in his spiritual notes: "the self of the universal is not the self of anything else" (127). The uniqueness of the self can also be its burden, and the Terrible Sonnets emphasize this burden, the loneliness of the self. However, in three of his later poems, the persona renews the attempt to relate himself to the reader. In "Harry Ploughman" (Sept. 1887), the tentative surfacing of the artist, involved not only with his subject but also with the reader, is indicated by the imperatives "look" and "see." The persona is inviting the reader to share his experience, to witness the beauty and strength of Harry inscaped in the act of ploughing. Moving out of his own self, the poet-persona again becomes aware of "the other self"—Harry Ploughman, the subject of his observation and the reader, the addressee. The poem begins with no reference to the reader; only when the poet begins to observe Harry acting out his beauty and strength is the reader called in. The intensity of the moment, its significance to the persona who, in the dark sonnets, had felt the alienation of the ploughman (common man, self as poet and priest) from his plough, eases the bridging of the persona-reader distance.

In "St. Alphonsus Rodriguez" (composed around October 1888),[18] the shared identity of the persona and the reader, "we," is placed in the larger framework of the common man (106). Once the persona has established communication with the reader, the ensuing unified self, "we," takes the final leap to relate itself to the third entity of the rhetorical triangle, the subject. Here the subject of the poem is the common man. The persona, perhaps a failure in the world of events, does re-enact Christ who "could crowd career with conquest" in his inner struggle at self-discovery and communication with other selves.

In "The Shepherd's Brow," the interlocked identities of persona/reader/-subjecthood achieve an artistic significance. The history of its appearance among Hopkins' published works throws some light on the shifts that have taken place in the critical assessment of its importance. Robert Bridges had refused to include this poem among Hopkins' finished poems because of its "cynical mood," and so did W. H. Gardner until the fourth edition of *The Poems of Gerard Manley Hopkins*. In their notes to the poem in the fourth edition, Gardner and MacKenzie emphasized that Hopkins is "stressing man's essential limitations" in the poem. They analyze line twelve as follows:

> The aposiopesis is obviously deliberate and seems to mark the culmination of disgust: "And I that...but why mention my own earnestness? Life is a grotesque masquerade of inverted or distorted images, and my own trials and tantrums are equally unheroic." (296)

With Robert Boyle, S.J., Sr. Mary Campbell, Robert Clark, S.J., and Paul L. Mariani, there came a rush of critical assessment of the poem as a finished and complex work of art.[19] Mary Campbell's conclusion is noteworthy (here she is referring to the third edition of Gardner's *The Poems*):

> The sonnet is not a simple one, and among its most interesting complexities is precisely that of tone: it passes from admiration through indignation and the deepest disgust and pain to a most sincere humility and quiet. This alone should redeem it from its status, in Gardner's edition, in the last page of the "fragments."(142)

The persona, in the mood of the last poems, views "Man Jack's pretense to greatness seen in the unflattering light of his essential smallness" (Mariani, "Artistic and Tonal" 68). In the world of ordinary daily life, the three selves, those of the poet, the reader and the common man (the subject of the poem), are but brittle bones. But does art in some way affect their identity? Thomas K. Beyette's analysis in this context is helpful to a certain extent. In "Hopkins' Phenomenology of Art in 'The Shepherd's Brow,'" he discusses Hopkins' problem of artistic creation:

> The subject of Hopkins' "The Shepherd's Brow" is, then, the double-edged problem of artistic creativity. The poet not only faces up to the lack of epic or tragic material available in common man or personal experience but also encounters the artistic problem of accommodating inspiration to a poetic shape that will faithfully convey its import. (212)[20]

The ambiguity of the word "tame" in the second last line of the poem opens one to that quality of artistic creation discussed before—the transformation of self. Beyette's analysis refers to taming of the fire of artistic inspiration in the mirror of art:

> In any event, the "smooth spoons" of Hopkins' sonnets "feed this flame" or add to the blazoned story of common man, including himself, but at the same time "tame the poet's "tempests"—his inspiration mirrored in poetry-as well as his inspirational "fire" and "fever fussy." "Tame" is also in a way characteristic of Hopkins, an adjective as well as a verb; that is, in the mirror of art the poet's "tempest" or "fever" appears tame-a reflected pale fire. (212)

Tamed," however, can also be interpreted as "controlled," especially when we consider that it is not the "fire and fever fussy" of the Jack self, but that of the poet-persona which is being "tamed" by the artistic creation. The poet-persona had started off by associating himself with the reader and the common man who share the same breath from childhood to old age, but in line nine the "we" is divided into the "He" and "I." Paul L. Mariani, in

"The Artistic and Tonal Integrity of Hopkins' 'The Shepherd's Brow'," points out this association:

> But it will be noted that Hopkins who had identified himself with man in lines five ("we") and eight ("our"), in line nine contemptuously dissociates himself from Man Jack with an emphatic "He!" Having set up a comparison between Man Jack, undistinguished by his generically undifferentiated "manmarks," and the distinctively individuating "sakes" of God's lightening on his shepherd and the fallen angels, Hopkins, in line twelve, isolates himself above the Jacks to plead his own particular case, his own sake, his intensely personal agony. (65)

In "smooth spoons," that is, art, the reflection of his life appears a comical, distorted masque, unfit for high tragedy. Hopkins' persona is aware of his own smallness, but unlike the Man Jack he acknowledges it; he expresses it in words, and this very expression becomes his hope for recovery. From this state of humility, he can create an art that is in consonance with his renewed awareness of self, an art that "tames" or "controls" the subject of the chaos of his struggles. Disillusioned by the absurdity of modern man as a subject for high tragedy and the reality of common existence, he wishes for an art which will help tone down the extremities of his "tempests," his "fire and fever fussy." At this point, he does not wish for art's magical transformation that he had earlier believed in and had captured in the moments of inscape and instress. Felix Randal, in reality, was broken by sickness, but in art, in the persona's inscapes, the banality and pain of human suffering were transformed. In "The Shepherd's Brow" the poet-persona faces the reality of what art can do and what it cannot. Here the poet wishes for an art that would help one take a measured look at human life. In another sense too, art can tame one's tempests; in creating art one moves out of one's own pitiful self and all its feverish concerns (expressed in the Terrible Sonnets), out of the density of common man who is "to his own selfbent so bound," ("Ribblesdale," 90) to communicate with the other self. In this state of symbiosis, each self must unite with the other. Superficially, this sense of art's significance seems opposed to Hopkins' belief in creating individual inscapes in poetry. However, what the persona wishes to be toned down in art is not the beauty or mark of the individual self but its self-lacerations, its self-indulged importance, its grime and its shame. What he wants toned down, finally, is those qualities of the self which separate man and Christ. The poem read in this light evolves into a significant response. But it is markedly devoid of the paeonic assertion, of magical poetic transformation. Having faced one's own jaded self, Hopkins' persona withholds, in the last phase of his evolution, the exuberance of surrender to untested faith assumptions, even as he refrains from anxious self-accusations. W. H. Gardner compares him to the Hamlet figure: "This is not the smiling, aloof cynicism of La Rochefoucauld but the bitter self-implicated cynicism of Hamlet—the cry of the disappointed idealist" (v. 1, 65). However, for Hopkins, despite its inadequacies art does effect a change in the self's understanding of its condition. Paul Mariani's comment regarding "To R.B." in "The Sound of Oneself Breathing" is relevant in this context as well:

> What the last poem tells us, then, is that Hopkins has come to accept his very human condition....Ironically for the first (and last) time in poetry, the density of anxious fretting in the introspective sonnets has lifted. One senses that Hopkins has come to accept himself, the apparent failure signalled by his long poetic silences, but the movement of the Spirit as well, operating within as it will. Affective and elective wills have for once meshed. The voice in this song is aware of the cost of the silence to one's poetic reputation, aware, but willing without anxiousness for once to pay the price. For once, then: something. (25-26)

Worked out from the persona's self-depreciation, disappointment and cynicism to a kind of self-composure, the poem salvages something out of the chaos of the human condition. If we choose to live merely "hand to mouth," human insignificance can become the link between individual selves, and Hopkins' later poetry confronts this possibility. That is why we, as readers, are struck by the grit and grim picture of the "Jack" self. However, in art, as in priestly work, Hopkins found the substance for human interaction and communication. Often he felt thwarted in his efforts, his lines "lagging" ("To R. B.," 108), himself as "Time's eunuch," and if in these last poems one notes the dominance of cynicism, one cannot but be aware of the poet's genuine attempts at creating the ideal community. Even as the priest-persona struggled to sympathize with the parish figures, the poet-persona sought the community of the reader and finally of the human lot. In priestly duties and in poetic work, he affirmed the growing relationships among the self, the other and God.

Notes

1. St. Ignatius Loyola, *The Spiritual Excercises*, trans.David L. Fleming,, S. J. (St. Louis: The Institute of Jesuit Sources, 1978) 16, 18.

2. Donald Walhout, *Send My Roots Rain* (Athens: Ohio University Press, 1981) 24-48.

3. W. H. Gardner and N. H. MacKenzie, eds., *The Poems of Gerard Manley Hopkins*, 4th ed. (New York: Oxford University Press, 1967) 100, 98.
   Note: All quotes from Hopkins' poems are cited from the above text and will subsequently be indicated by page numbers in parenthesis.

4. Bell Gale Chevigny, "Instress and Devotion in the Poetry of Gerard Manley Hopkins,"*Victorian Studies* 9 (1965): 145.

5. William B. Thesing, "'Tom's Garland' and Hopkins' Inscapes of Humanity," *Victorian Poetry* 15 (Spring 1977): 37.

6. Norman H. MacKenzie, *A Reader's Guide to Gerard Manley Hopkins* (Ithaca: Cornell University Press, 1981) 179.

7. James Finn Cotter, *Inscape* (Pittsburgh: University of Pittsburgh Press, 1972) 288-89.

8. W. H. Gardner, *Gerard Manley Hopkins (1844-1889): A Study of Poetic Idiosyncracy in Relation to Poetic Tradition*, vol. 1 (New Haven: Yale University Press, 1948) 11-12.

9. John Wain, "An Idiom of Desperation," *Hopkins: A Collection of Critical Essays*, ed. Geoffrey H. Hartman (New Jersey: Prentice-Hall, 1966) 64-65.

10. Claude Colleer Abbott, ed., *The Letters of Gerard Manley Hopkins to Robert Bridges* (London: Oxford University Press, 1935) 170.

11. J. Hillis Miller, "The Theme of the Disappearance of God in Victorian Poetry,"*Victorian Studies* 6 (Mar. 1963): 224.

12. Gerard Manley Hopkins, "On Principium sive Fundamentum: Comments on the Spiritual Excercises of St. Ignatius Loyola," *The Notebooks and Papers of Gerard Manley Hopkins*, ed. Humphrey House (London: Oxford University Press, 1937) 317.

13 Joseph Eble, "Levels of Awareness: A Reading of Hopkins' 'Felix Randal,'" *Victorian Poetry* 13 (1975): 131-132.

14 John Sutherland, "'Tom's Garland': Hopkins' Political Poem," *Victorian Poetry* 10 (1972): 115.

15 Robert Bernard Martin, *Gerard Manley Hopkins: A Very Private Life* (London: Harper Collins, 1991) 329.

16 C. Day Lewis, *The Poetic Image* (London: Oxford University Press, 1947) 126.

17 Jess Stein, ed., *The Random House College Dictionary*, revised ed. (New York: Random House, 1979) 457.

18 W. H. Gardner and N. H. MacKenzie, eds., "Notes," *The Poems of Gerard Manley Hopkins*, 4th ed., 295.

19 Robert Boyle, S. J., *Metaphor in Hopkins* (Chapel Hill, 1961); Robert B. Clark, S. J., "Hopkins' 'The Shepherd's Brow,'" *Victorian Newsletter* 28 (Fall 1965): 16-18; Sr. M. Mary Hugh Campbell, S.C.M.M., "The Silent Sonnet: Hopkins' 'Shepherd's Brow,'" *Renascence* 15 (Spring 1963): 133-142; Paul L. Mariani, "The Artistic and Tonal Integrity of Hopkins' 'The shepherd's Brow,'" *Victorian Poetry* 6 (Spring 1968): 63-68, and "The Sound of Oneself Breathing: The Burden of Theological Metaphor in Hopkins," *The Hopkins Quarterly* 4.1 (Spring 1977): 19-26.

20 Thomas K. Beyette, "Hopkins' Phenomenology of Art in 'The Shepherd's Brow,'" *Victorian Poetry* 11 (1973): 212.

Chapter 3

Between the Miraculous and the Quotidian: Francis Thompson, the Visionary Poet

Francis Thompson's poetry records the fantasies and failures of a double vision, those of a child and of an old man, even as they are played out on a double stage, that of the heavens and the streets. As a man in his thirties he could fling out with the abandonment of the very young, "Look for me in the nurseries of Heaven," and as a man in his forties he was to die with the self-regret of the very old, "My withered life, my withered life!" (Walsh 216).[1] In a short span of poetic creativity, Francis Thompson lived and died with the nonchalant petulance of a spirit that creates miracles if it does not see one and with the soul-weariness of a body racked by drug addiction, ill health and indolence.

Often contrived and extravagant in his poetic style, Francis Thompson today survives as a "minor" poet on the basis of a handful of poems. Studied as a literary figure emerging from the upheavals of political, social and literary history, Thompson is often placed alongwith a coterie of Catholic poets attempting Catholic literary revival. Yet, his poetry, with its theological metaphors and subjects, is not concerned with the kind of religious conflicts and struggles we find expressed in Newman and Hopkins. One explanation is that Thompson was a product of a generation that had already converted to Catholicism, unlike Newman and Hopkins who chose their Church out of a nexus of social, ideological, spiritual, emotional and personal pressures. They needed to give utterance to the immediately felt convictions of faith, of self-torment, guilt and keenly fought triumphs. Thompson accepted the Catholic theology and translated its rituals, its theocracy and symbolism into his writings as a matter of fact. This ease in handling Catholic material gives his poems such as "The Hound of Heaven," "Grace of the Way," "Any Saint," "Desiderium

Indesideratum," and "Kingdom of God" a strikingly confident sense of self's recovery, whatever the nature of its initial backward glances. But it also robs his poetry of a quality the modern reader has come to appreciate—the internal struggle, as in "Sister Songs," "Ode to the Setting Sun," "The Passion of Mary," and "Orient Ode."[2] This kind of poetry does not jolt the reader or cause "the midriff astrain with leaning of" as experienced in reading Hopkins' poems. Here, Thompson's struggle, told not enacted, seems too facile to us, even as strained as his poetic style was. No doubt, much of his poetry and prose writing was journalistic, with comparisons, images, and feelings contrived in order to "get the opportunity of dropping in two or three 'bits'" (Walsh 31).[3] Lacking a defined poetic theory or even a conviction of his own poetic standards, Thompson drifted into poetic writing in a haze of laudanum-induced poems. Until reading Alice Meynell's poems, he was not even sure of his own poetic capability. He constantly needed a push from the outside to make himself move to mental or physical activity, as evidenced in his passive acceptance of the vocations chosen by his parents—priesthood and medicine. Other evidences are his dependence on the unknown woman in the streets, on the Meynells and others who cared and nursed him (referred to in "Sister Songs"), and on Patmore whom he considered his literary mentor (reflected in his poems and letters to Patmore and to Wilfrid Meynell). This dependence of self on others defines the quantity and nature of Thompson's poetic subject matters: there are several poems written on the Meynell family (Wilfrid, Alice and their children), on the lost woman of his dreams, and on Patmore. This is not to say Thompson was insincere in his choice of subjects for his poetry, but that he was convinced to do so because these external factors gave direction and substance to his otherwise exiled existence.

Francis Thompson's poetry and writing reveal one interesting development in the late nineteenth century. While Hopkins recaptured the miraculous in the inscapes of ordinary natural and human objects, Thompson's flights into the cosmic playground are not won through "sheer plod." Thompson's miracles are not always won through self-torment and self-appraisal as Hopkins' are. Thompson's miracles exist even as his "box of toys" and the "theatrical puppetdom" existed in his childhood, as recorded by Everard Meynell in *The Life of Francis Thompson* (Meynell 8).[4] These miracles do not need any justification, nor does the self batter itself and God by questioning its own worth and worthlessness for viewing such miracles. Thompson's writing, in consonance with his life, thus records the realm of the miraculous as a self-existent world. As the dark streets of London exist, so the heavens with star-marbles for "little Jesus" exist. It is only when Thompson brings together the two planes of existence, when he breaks the extremity of his vision, when he collapses the heavens and the London streets into the "labyrinthine" ways of the self, when he sees "Jacob's ladder/Pitched betwixt Heaven and Charing Cross" and "Christ walking on the water/Not of Gennesareth, but Thames" that he sees the miraculous and the quotidian not as separate realms of existence but as related worlds, linking scriptural truths and human experience. These instances are rare in Thompson's poetry, but when they do occur, they are as striking as Hopkins' poems. My analysis is not meant to merely salvage Thompson's worth as a late-nineteenth-century poet, but to re-evaluate those poems which actualize the failure to integrate the heavens and the streets, the miraculous and the quotidian in terms of autobiographical details and reader-response, as they operate within the parameters of cultural imperatives. These poems are particularly relevant because they reveal in Thompson's poetry the emergence of and the divergence from the spirit that was to characterize the poetry of Lionel Johnson, Oscar Wilde, Ernest Dowson, and even W. B. Yeats—the spirit of decadence. My attempt in this chapter is to read and respond to Francis Thompson's poems that express a dual pull, towards and away from Hopkins' and the decadents'.

In his biography of Thompson, *The Life of Francis Thompson*, Everard Meynell points out the double rule of Thompson's practice: "'to the Poet life is full of visions, to the mystic it is one vision.' Having regarded the visions and set them down, he would, in another capacity, call them in. The vision enfolded them all" (201). Within the broad framework of the cosmic vision, Thompson was concerned particularly with the nature of the God-man relationship. In Thompson's vision of love, man's relationship with the human and the divine are discovered at various levels; in his vision of poetic creation, Thompson confronted the soul's relationship to its own creative self and to God. In examining these visions, not as separate entities but as corresponding and interacting searchings of the soul, one can gather three different states: the untrained state of the vision, the failure of the vision in actual human experiences, and the emergence of the new vision or the transformation of the old vision. The attempt is not to neatly categorize the poems but to understand the poetic expressions (such as the "dropping down" of the "curbed spirit," v. I, 77, 83; and the "up-thrusting, "skyward-jetting soul," v. I, 60, 82) in terms of the responses they evoke in the context of the reading experience.

Many of Thompson's poems which deal with the God-man relationship seem, at first, to be based on a contradictory vision of God. They also reveal a dual vision of the self. In some poems like "To My Godchild," "Sister Songs," "Ode to the Setting Sun," "To the Dead Cardinal of Westminister," "The Veteran of Heaven," "Lilium Regis," "A Sunset," "Song of the Heavens," "The Dread of Height," "Orient Ode," "From the Night of Forebeing," "To the English Martyrs" and "Heaven and Hell," God's distance from man is felt by the persona as a palpable experience. A sense of man's separateness from God is built up through a response to various stylistic, tonal, structural, rhetorical and philosophic features in the poems. In some poems, God's remoteness is worked into the substance of language and results in a felt remoteness of diction, imagery and formality of tone, echoing the language from scriptural and literary tradition. In poems like "Lilium Regis," "Ode to the Setting Sun," "The Orient Ode," "Ad Castitatem," and "Assumpta Maria," there is actual evocation of imagery from the Holy Scripture and the Catholic liturgical and mystical tradition. In "The Orient Ode," the liturgical pattern reflected in the sacramental vision of the sun as the Host consecrated in Benediction is elaborate and sustained. Christ, who is symbolized as the sun and as the Lion of Judah, is also the "destroyer and preserver" out of a literary and a Catholic tradition (Thompson v. II, 21-23). The response he evokes in Thompson and other creatures is one of mingled fear, awe and longing. Here the persona emphasizes man's littleness before God's immensity, grandeur and splendour, even as the chorus in "The Song of the Hours" warns man: "God breathes you forth as a bubble/And shall suck you back into his mouth!" (v. I, 209).

The critical objections to Thompson's elaborate diction and imagery range from Alice Meynell, who called them "ceremonies of imagination," to J. C. Reid, who finds in this poem "a startling resemblance to the verse of the Spasmodics, who also present vague, cosmic vistas in inflated, repetitive language, grandiosely use all space as their stage and deal in large-sounding 'poetic' images (107).[5] It is these very "faults" in language, style and imagery which build up to a picture of the distant God who inflicts pain and suffering on man. The lack of direct confrontation between God and the self is heightened by rhetorical structures in which the persona addresses a third "other" to intercede between himself and the absent God. Appearing "the happy Fool of Christ," the self like the "Dear Jester in the courts of God" finds he is unable to reach his King, Christ:

But I, ex-Paradised
The shoulder of your Christ Find high
To lean thereby.
        ("To the Dead Cardinal," V. I, 132)

Mystified by the "secret terrible," the mystery of God's loving acceptance of man, he prays to his friend Cardinal Manning to intervene. In "Sing, Bird Sing" from *The Man Has Wings*, the self reaches God through kinship with the singing bird (Connolly, ed. 55).[6] A final break from the remote God and his entourage (pictured as old, bearded men in artistic and religious renderings) is expressed in "To My Godchild." The persona wishes to be in the company of the god who is young and playful—another child: "Look for me in the nurseries of Heaven" (v. I, 18-19).

Another rhetorical devise used to create the effect of distance between the self and God is obvious in the poem, "The Veteran of Heaven." Imaged as a warrior, Christ is addressed by the persona as "O Captain of the wars," "Strange chief," and is referred to as "ye" not "you." These titles and formal salutations place God on a plane where even his suffering is awe-inspiring, rather than immediately felt ("The Veteran of Heaven," v. I, 149). In other poems, such as "From the Night of Forebeing," isolation or limitation of self, the "stagnation" of the spirit, indirectly suggests the unbridgeable gap between the cosmic reality and the quotidian self (v. II, 41). A modernist expression of the isolation of self from God is nowhere more poignantly expressed by Thompson's persona than in the poem "The Dread of Height":

My soul with anguish and recoil
Doth like a city in an earthquake rock
(v. II, 20)

The persona whose "conquered skies do grow a hollow mock" is the inhabitor of the quotidian world, of the "city in an earthquake rock" whose "streets...on the utmost glittering day are black" (v. III, 52). Yet, in other poems, the persona-self is "native to high heaven." Here the nearness of God to man and his accessibility are emphasized. The abundance of emotionally-charged metaphors, images, simplicity of style and language (compared to the highly wrought technique characteristic of Thompson), direct addresses to God, and a sense of self's peace with itself and God, all work to create the loving bond of God-man relationship. Most of these poems begin with a child's faith in God's loving concern and are often marked by a charming naiveté. Sometimes, in playful questioning, the child-self of the persona replaces the given image of God as an old bearded man with that of another child:

> Little Jesus, wast thou shy
> Once, and just so small as I?
> And what did it feel like to be
> Out of Heaven, and just like me?
> ("Little Jesus," v. I, 21)

Seeking identification with "Little Jesus," the persona establishes grounds for companionship. The self-confident tone, the repetition of questions and the simplicity of language are effectively controlled. Besides addressing Jesus directly, the persona invites him, "Take me by the hand and walk" (22). Holding hands, a simple gesture in itself, evokes the relationship of friendship and love; it is also a recurring motif in poems that celebrate this human-divine bond on a personal level. In "Love and the Child," as in "The Hound of Heaven," the persona's stubborn resistance to the clasping arms of God is broken when he perceives God not as the punishing but as the loving, tender father (v. I, 175). In "Any Saint," God's nearness and his humbleness are in explicit contrast to the image of Christ with unreachable shoulders, as represented in "To the Dead Cardinal of Westminister":

> And bolder now and bolder
> I lean upon that shoulder,
>   So dear
> He is and near . . .
>   (v. II, 45)

The persona "blent/In wished content" with his "gentle lover" at first seeks the familiar image of God as the taskmaster, thus delaying the confrontation with an abundance of love which he does not know how to accept at this point:

> Turn something of Thy look,
> And fear me with rebuke,
>   That I
> May timorously

> Take tremors in Thy arms
> ("Any Saint," v. II, 46)

The persona's words like "fear," "rebuke," "timorously," and "tremors" echo the choric warning in "Song of the Hours," but all the familiar images of God as "wrathful spear" and "thunder-spout" dwindle in the moment of the persona's embrace with God. Within the circle of that embrace the persona learns to accept and give love:

> Rise; for Heaven hath no frown
> When thou to thee pluck'st down,
>   Strong clod!
>   The neck of God. (51)

On the other hand, "The Passion of Mary" is quite formal and constrained in its tone and traditional in its imagery. Until the fourth stanza, the persona is addressing "Lady Mary," and imagining her sorrow. It is in the fourth stanza that the persona becomes aware of himself, a distinct self which by emotional empathy partakes of Mary's sorrow:

> Thy Son went up the angel's ways,
> His passion ended; but, ah me!
> *Thou* found'st the road of further days
>   A longer way of Calvary
>   (171)

The emotionally charged, self-reflexive "but, ah me!" is an instance of the persona's involvement, on a personal level, with the very texture of religious history so characteristic of Hopkins (see "The Wreck of the Deutschland," stanza eight: "Ah, touched in your bower of bone/Are you!").[7] Unlike Hopkins' persona, however, Thompson's stops short of searching self-analysis. As the poem develops, the instance of personal response is dispersed in a more generalized ("chills our mirth" as against "but, ah me!"), evocation of the traditional symbols of the "Assumption of our Lady" and the "Ascension of the Resurrected Body of Her Divine Son."[8] Finally, in "L'Envoy," the persona's self-consolation through the identification of his sadness with Mary's "Christian sadness" is strained and stylized, even as the imagery is sentimental and prosaic:

> The salt tears in our life's dark wine
>   Fell in it from the saving cross.
>   ("L'Envoy," v. 1, 72)

The point is not that all symbolism drawn from religious or literary tradition need be general, but without a personal significance given to the symbol, its potential remains undiscovered. The symbol drawn from tradition is rich in associations, but if the poet does not bring to it the substance of his/her own personal and emotional experience, it becomes distanced especially for readers in more secular periods of time. In most of Hopkins' poems using religious symbolism, the persona "I" is present at the experiential core of the poem. A look at one such poem, "The Blessed Virgin Compared to the Air We Breathe," confirms this observation. It is not so much the comparison of Virgin Mary with air that is striking. As observed by Norman MacKenzie,

> The Virgin has down the ages been represented by innumerable images, such as Noah's dove, the Ark of the Covenant, Star of the Sea, the Sheep that bore the Lamb of God and the Church's Diadem. Here Hopkins develops with skill some metaphors for Mary in various famous hymns in the Divine Office— "the portal of heaven" or "the gateway through which light arose over the earth": in having given birth to the light of the world she is like the air which transmits sunshine and acts as intermediary between earth and heaven. Mary's traditional colour, blue, favoured the image, which Hopkins had already used in a sermon on 5 October 1879 (*Sermons*, 29). (157)[9]

It is not so much "Mary's role as the spiritual mother of mankind" that is at the core of the poem, but its significance to the persona at the moment of his discovery of its actual relevance to him. The emphasis on "I," "me" and "my" draw the reader into direct contact with an experiencing persona who relives the religious symbol as a personal truth, not merely as a given tradition.

Francis Thompson's more complex, and in a sense, more rewarding poems are those which avoid viewing the God-man relationship either as destined to failure or as one of easy sympathy. These poems particularly stand out as coalescing the two voices into a vision of faith in the human self and in God. In "A Judgement in Heaven," the movement from a picture of a regal but distant God to that of a loving and gentle Father is worked out through an intermediary. It is Mary Magdalen who draws the rhymer-poet persona to God's attention. The rhetorical structure operating here is dramatic repetition, not of words but of a pattern of command and action. Mary's sentences, cast in the imperative mood, almost take on a choric effect: "'Turn yon robe,' spake Magdalen 'of torn bright/song, and see and feel,'" "'Take, I pray, yon chaplet up, thrown down ruddied/from his head'" (v. I, 189). Each of these commands is fulfilled by the angels, revealing the hidden sufferings of the poet-persona's life. God has till now been a silent audience to the unfolding of the drama. Here God, unlike the pursuing "Hound of Heaven," needs to be convinced of the persona's suffering. The poet, "a dingy creature," "cloaked and clad in patchwork things," the rhymer's garb, is no doubt a poor and sinful figure, but then God, enthroned in his Paradise, king of "His aged dominions," is not directly approachable to the poet-rhymer. Till now the man-God relationship has been one of an erring, wretched servant and his majestic king, surrounded by scornful angels and warden-spirits. But in the last stanza, God speaks. The reader anticipates God's words to be uttered in a loud, authoritative tone, and reads the line in declarative mood "'Fetch forth the Paradisal garb!'" as such. But the anticipation breaks even as the line continues in indicative mood, "Spake the Father,/sweet and low." The adverbs "sweet and "low," added almost casually, catch the reader's attention and direct a revision of the line's initial reading. This difference between expectation and actuality comes as a surprise to the reader, even as it does to the poor poet-persona waiting for all thunder to break lose. Dramatically worked into the structure and the experience of the poem, the new vision is marked by the simple gesture of hand-holding (189).

Thompson's collection of poems seems to present, at first reading, a dual vision of the God-man relationship—a vision which is contradictory and sometimes paradoxical. It is in later readings that one comes to emphasize the place of "The Hound of Heaven" as central to the evolving nature of Thompson's cosmic vision. In "The Hound of Heaven," the God-man relationship is discovered through God's pursuit of man. Whereas in "A Judgement in Heaven" the poet-rhymer had come to God's court, seeking his grace, here God pursues man through the streets and alleys of the quotidian world. God rushes man from self-deception to self-confrontation, to a vision of the God-man relationship. From the terrifying view of God and man as inhabitors of two separate worlds, the persona escapes into an unreal vision of himself. As an entity of the quotidian world, the persona is solipsistic ("I fled Him, down the labyrinthine ways/Of my own mind") and, in the context of Victorian standards of morality, dissipated ("I pleaded, outlaw wise,/By many a hearted casement, curtained red"). As an entity of the miraculous realm, the persona builds up an image of himself as an innocent companion of children and of nature (108, 109). These visions of the persona-self, however, neither "ease" the "human smart"nor "slake" his "drouth." The moment of the persona's recognition of the falsity of the vision of self, its divisive nature and its extremity, is also the moment of self-confrontation and its failures: "Yea, faileth now even dream/The dreamer, and the lute the lutanist" (111). It is marked by a series of questions and doubts hurled at God, by a last minute attempt to salvage some self-worth through self-pity. Although he had declared "Naked I wait Thy love's uplifted stroke!" the persona is not yet ready to face his own worthlessness:

Ah! must Thou char the wood ere Thou canst limn
   with it?

> ...
> Such is; what is to be?
> The pulp so bitter, how shall taste the rind?
>   (111)

These questionings are drowned in the "trumpet sounds" heralding what appears to be a regal personage "enwound/With glooming robes purpureal, cypress-crowned." Even then, the persona, full of self-pity, tries to put in the last words. It is only in the resounding voice of God that the persona's complaints, questionings, and doubts disperse. In himself, on earth, man is seen as nothing but the "dingiest clot," "little worthy of love." It is only by taking God's hand that the persona understands the nature of the God-man relationship. Even as the Christ of miraculous heavens came down to earth, so man of the quotidian world can rise to heaven. By reciprocating God's embrace, the "fondest, blindest, weakest" persona-self is able to build a new vision of himself and his relation to God. In the last stanza, the persona, however, is addressed by God as "child," but is no longer an innocent (ignorant) entity of the "miraculous world." God's chiding tone reduces the persona (the man-self) to his rightful status, yet this is not a mere ego-straightening exercise. Rather, the persona's recognition of his true habitation as lying between the miraculous and the quotidian relieves him of his lonely wandering like an exile. The realm of the persona-self, shaded by "His hand, outstretched carressingly," is his comfort and solace—his community.

The theme of God's pursuit of man's soul has been a recurrent concern in spiritual struggles, whether recorded by St. Ignatius Loyola in *The Spiritual Exercises* or by St. Augustine in his *Confessions*: "But behold, Thou wert close behind Thy fugitives—at once God of venegeance and Fountain of mercies, who turnest us to Thyself by wondrous means" (47).[11] From these and other sources of spiritual struggle, Hopkins had evolved a highly personal version of the God-man relationship. A study of his "The Wreck of Deutschland" at this point reveals an interesting development of a vision, sometimes similar and sometimes different from Francis

Thompson's. In this poem, God's pursuit of man, whether the poet or the drowning nuns, is enacted not merely as a horizontal movement. The persona's self or soul is overwhelmed with God's presence as God pursues the soul from all sides, in all ways. The results of the confrontation of the self with the relentless, pursuing God are worked out in stanzas four and five. The persona-self realizes that he is both controlled in and controls the expression of his inscape. The self also realizes that its spiritual equilibrium is sustained by "God's gift," grace (*PGMH* 52). The final outcome is the persona's spontaneous attempts to actualize Christ's incarnation in experiential terms, "His mystery must be instressed, stressed" (*PGMH* 53).

In Hopkins' poetry the self, pursued by God, returns to him even as it does in Thompson's "The Hound of Heaven," but there is a difference. In Thompson's poem, the persona as the child-self, chided lovingly by God, finds comfort within his arms. The innocence and the transgression of the child-self are fused into the prodigal's abashed willingness to stay home. In Hopkins' poem, the persona, flinging himself to the "heart of the Host," is stilled to spiritual poise. But even as the soft sand and the water in the well, while being under control and "roped" down, express motion, so the poised self expresses God's mystery with a kiss to "the stars." The pursuing figure who confronted the persona from behind, above and front, is now expressed as being "under" the wondrous mystery of the world's beauty. It is the persona who willingly completes the awareness of God's pervasiveness. It is this recognition of God as the self's underlying foundation, as "Ground of being, and granite of it" (*PGMH* 62), which uplifts the persona into ecstatic celebration.

In Francis Thompson's poem, "The Hound of Heaven," the persona finds the median, the comforting home between the fantasies and the streets. The persona reaches his place of rest and, in a way, the end of his past life. The poem closes on this note of an end of a journey. In Hopkins' poem, "The Wreck of Deutschland," the persona-self never rests for long. He is effusive in the celebration of his homecoming to "the heart of the Host." The persona's inner poise is not a state of stasis; it defies stillness with motion, death with life. No longer swooning down to flee the pursuer, but freely communing with the stars and the sky, instressing Christ's mystery, the new self of the persona reaches the heights of spiritual ecstacy. This is characteristic of Hopkins' poetry: from depths of despair he is able to rise to the heights. It is this convolution or evolution of the persona-self that binds the reader's attention. In her seminal book on reader-response aesthetics, Louise M. Rosenblatt refers to seeing the work of art as a special kind of lived-through experience, by quoting Keats' "On Sitting Down to Read *Kinq Lear* Once Again" and by commenting on it,

> "... once again, the fierce dispute Betwixt damnation and impassion'd clay, Must I burn through."
> The special mark of the literary work of art is indeed that it is "burned through," lived through, by a reader. (27)[12]

The intensity and dynamism of the persona-self in its relation to God, so profoundly captured again and again by Hopkins, give its moments of rest and poise a poignancy. It is felt by the reader, even as the persona experiences it, as a wrenching of the very soul.

Thompson's "The Hound of Heaven" is self-contained; the experience of the persona is unified and complete. An instance of spiritual composure attained through a process of self-deception, struggle and self-revelation, "The Hound of Heaven" records a genuinely felt faith in God's grace and man's destiny. The suffering of the quotidian man, expressed as "charred wood" and "broken fount" is a reflection of the hopelessness of human destiny. On the other hand, the miraculous "trumpet-sounds/From the hid battlements of Eternity" seem to emphasize God as a remote sovereign. Thompson expresses a synthesis of the two visions at the end of "The Hound of Heaven" and successfully translates the crux of Christian theology into the individual's experience of God's abundant love. Later poems that reaffirm this simple faith, though not as well known as "The Hound of Heaven," are equally striking in their emotional composure and strength of belief.

In "Grace of the Way," God-man's "trysting place" is not the suffering, commonplace world in "Thompson's 'Grace of the Way'," George Williams explicates the poem in the light of what he calls "Thompson's gentle and loving theology":

> Considered as a whole, the poem (as in the better known "The Hound of Heaven" and in many other of Thompson's works) expresses the belief that the way to God is easy, that it is simpler to have God than not to have Him, that happiness comes from having God, and sorrow comes from not having Him....In plain prose, then, Thompson would say: "God does not establish any strange place of sorrow and suffering—uncongenial both to man and to God, and quite uncharacteristic of God's kingdom—as a spot where man's feet shall seek out a meeting with God. Christ suffered on a tree; man need not so suffer. Rather, the way to God is a *"sweet* Direction." Neverthless [in the final stanza] it happens that some people fail to find God, yet find suffering, and think because they have suffered [the lesson] they have met God [the prize]. (16-17)[13]

In the poem, the persona's soul meets God through the mediating "she" (who is like the bodiless paramour of "Sister Songs" and "The Mistress of Vision"):

> Out of this abject earth of me
> I was translated and enskied
>   Into the heavenly-regioned She.
>   (v. II, 67)

Her direction to the "trysting-place" leads to the actual meeting, marked by God's humbleness and graciousness to stoop to his level. In the sonnet "Desiderium Indesideratum," the soul of the persona similarly discovers the accessibility of God who dwells in his own bosom as against the distant God of the heavens (v. II, 182). In "All Flesh," man's dilemma as both the inhabitor of the miraculous and the everyday world is emphasized. Like the earthly grass blade, man too epitomizes the mystery of God's presence—"God focussed to a point": "I am as God" (v. II, 225), but he is also imprisoned within his "clay-caught" self. In another sonnet, "House of Bondage," the common state of man, incapable of love or searching the wrong love (human) or searching love in wrong places (a remote Heaven, rather than his own heart), is viewed as man's "House of Bondage," a place where "The spirit's ark [is] sealed with a little clay" (179). In "The Kingdom of God," a similar image is used to describe the heart with "clay-shuttered doors" that misses "the many-splendoured thing" (226).

In this context, it is significant to elaborate on what Honnïghausen in *The Symbolist Tradition in English Literature* refers to as "Thompson's peculiar *fin de siècle* Catholicism" (140). The "trysting place" in the poem "The Kingdom of God" (v. II) can be seen as a variation of the garden motif that pervades the tradition of Pre-Raphaelite poetry until the fin de siècle as a specific outcome of the "theme of the tragic transcience of time" (138). As Honnïghausen observes, "for Francis Thompson the image of the garden clearly becomes the location for a transcendental experience" (140). Like the secret garden of "The Mistress of Vision," where the persona expresses his unique experience in terms of an anomaly, "Mine eyes saw not, and I saw," "the trysting place" becomes a symbol of spiritual refuge, in which man must willingly enter. Even as God sets up "no alien Tree," so man too must come to God, not with "estranged faces" nor with a heart of "clay-shuttered doors." The "trysting place" lies neither in the remote Heavens nor in the Charing Cross of "darkest England"; it lies somewhere in-between:

> and upon thy so sore loss
> Shall shine the traffic of Jacob's ladder
> Pitched betwixt Heaven and Charing Cross.
>   (226)

and it is here that man can define his own personally felt vision of "Heaven in Earth and God in Man":

> Yea, in the night, my soul, my daughter,

Cry,—clinging Heaven by the hems;
And lo, Christ walking on the water
Not of Gennesareth, but Thames!

(227)

ii

Francis Thompson's vision of the God-man relationship is related to a deeply felt need for two kinds of love—human and divine. At one level, this dual need is expressed as a dual search—the DeQuinceyan search for Ann, the woman of the streets and "the Lady of Sorrow," and the Shelleyan search for "pale Asthtaroth," the "visionary lady" or spiritual beauty. Thompson often expressed human love as a symbol of divine love:

> All human love was to me a symbol of divine love; nay, that human love was in my eyes a piteous failure unless as an image of the supreme Love which gave meaning and reality to its seeming insanity. (Meynell, *Life* 230)

In his poems of human love, whether for the woman of the streets or the visionary lady, Thompson rarely grappled with the different scales of physical and emotional responses. Not so much concerned with the "human" aspect of the love relationship, Thompson's poems of love are often reduced to an abstract spirituality too generally stated. His search for the "unknown she," "the bodiless paramour," started early, from the days of strolling through the Manchester museums and galleries. Enthralled by the cast of the Vatican Melpomene he wrote later in his essay, "The Fourth Order of Humanity":

> Wherefore, then, should I leave unmemorized the statue which enthralled my youth in a passion such as feminine mortality was skill-less to instigate? Nor at this let any boggle; for *she* was a goddess.
>
> (v. III, 68-69)

The response evoked by such a visionary lady is determined by her very nature and is much easier to tackle than the ambiguous response to the human complexity of blood and flesh woman who could deny him or condemn him with a gaze (69-70). This tendency to move away from a particular human experience to a more abstract contemplation of general truths and revelations are recurrent in Thompson. Very early in his poetry, Thompson's expression of love is mingled with a deep sense of loss. The pain of parting, at one instance, brings past and future losses to the mind:

> She went her unremembering way,
> She went and left in me
> The pang of all the partings gone,
> And partings yet to be.
>   ("Daisy," v. I, 4)

However, by the end of the poem the personal sorrow and the intensity of one human relationship is generalized as a universal truth:

> Nothing begins, and nothing ends,
> That is not paid with moan;
> For we are born in other's pain,
> And perish in our own. (5)

In "A Carrier Song" and "After her Going," from the sequence "Love in Dian's Lap," a similar sense of emptiness due to the absence of the loved person is caught in rhapsodizing tones (85, 103). In his letter to Wilfrid and Alice Meynell, who had visited him at Pantasaph, Thompson had written: "I think "the leaves fell from the day" indeed when your train went out of the station; and I never heard the birds with such bad voices (Walsh, ed. 117). This child-like dependence, especially on women, is characteristic of Thompson's poems of love as "the ambassador of loss" (20). The central experience in Thompson's life was his relationship with the unknown woman of the London streets. In "Sister Songs" and "Memorat Memoria" the persona relives the painful experience with a sense of loss, regret, self-inadequacy and marvel at the woman's sacrifice:

> She passed,—O brave, sad, lovingest, tender thing!
> And of her own scant pittance did she give,
>   That I might eat and live:
> Then fled, a swift and trackless fugitive
> 						("Sister Songs," v. I, 37)

In "Memorat Memoria" the memory of the loss of the loved one, "O shadow of a /Girl" is persistent and haunting (v. II, 216). The shift in the tone from the first lines to the last is striking. The repetitious echo of words as in a dizzying "whirl," and the emphasis on "I" and "me" reflect a highly personal expression of an equally personal experience. But the last line replaces "we" for "I" and the whole experience is again generalized. This tendency to generalize experiences related to actual women and deep feelings of sexual love is, in one sense, an escape mechanism. Generalization makes the palpable experience remote, and thus fit for contemplation rather than self-reflection and possible torment. In another sense, it helps him resolve the tension between the temporal aspect of human and divine love, the "pagan" and "Christian" love by merging the woman (Alice Meynell, Maggie Brien or Katie King) with the "Visionary Lady" (the "Vatican Melpomene," "the Mistress of Vision," the "bodiless paramour" or "Lady Mary" with the "Saint's and Mother's heart").

The divisive categories of woman reflect the binary view of the world in dichotomous terms: Christian/pagan, spiritual/physical, civilized/heathen. In his essay "Paganism Old and New," Thompson declared the nobility of the Christian poet's conception of Love:

> On the wings of Christianity came the great truth that Love is of the soul, and with the soul coeval....Therefore sings Dante, and sing all noble poets after him, that Love in this world is a pilgrim and a wanderer, a journeying to the New Jerusalem: not here is the consummation of his yearnings, in that mere knocking at the gates of union which we christian marriage, but beyond the pillars of death and the corridors of the grave, in the union of spirit to spirit within the containing Spirit of God. (v. III, 48)

In his poems occur several expressions of "spiritual" love: "bodiless paramour" ("Sister Songs," v. I, 43), "skyward-jetting soul" and "lofty love" ("Manus Animam Pinxit," v. I, 82, 83-84), "Heaven's Queen" ("A Carrier's Song" (v. I, 87), "pure lines" ("Orison Tryst," v. I, 201), "plentious graces" ("Ultima,". II, 93). The final union of self, the lady and God is expressed in "My Lady the Tyranness":

> None shall deny
> God to be mine, but He and I
> All yours, my love, all yours!
>   (Ultima," v. II, 98)

Other poems which deal with the particular experience of love also express a preplexed feeling of rejection, reflective of Thompson's own aborted love affairs with Maggie Brien and Katie King. In "Beginning of End" from the sequence, "A Narrow Vessel," the love expressed is more of an adolescent kind, hurting and being hurt out of egoistic motives. Left at the level of human falls and foibles, the poem escapes easy translation into spiritual terms despite Thompson's own attempts to allegorize it:

> The narrow vessel dreads to crack under the overflowing love which surges into it. She shrieks with tremor....Now this is but the image and explanation of the soul's attitude towards only God. The one is illustrated by the other....It falls back with relieved contentment on some human love, a love on its own plane, where somewhat short of total surrender may go to requital, where no upward effort is needful.
>   (Meynell, *Life* 231-32)

However, by the end of the sequence, Thompson's hesitation to deal with human love, as human, rounds off the whole sequence of "The Narrow Vessel" as an allegory, clearly expressed in the "Epilogue":

> She, that but giving part, not whole,
> Took even the part back, is the Soul   (v. II, 89)

The sonnets to Katie King, the "Ad Amicam" series, attempt to translate unfulfilled love into immortality through poetry. The sense of time separating two human beings, whether expressed as a passage of time or as a difference in ages, comes out of the literary "carpe diem" tradition Thompson was familiar with—particularly through Shakespeare. In "The Poppy" love is evoked as the "flower of withered dream" which is preserved from "reaper Time" within the "nook of rhyme" (v. I, 9).

In Thompson's poems, the emerging image of the persona-self central to the experience of human love is of more interest than the experience itself or even the object of love. At one level, there is the persona, conscious of his own self-image; at the other level, the reader must go beyond the persona's appearances and claims to understand the complexity of his personality and motives. The image of self as isolated from other human beings, an exile in an unfamiliar world, provides the motive for the persona's persistent yearnings for a love that transcends human limitations. On the other hand, the persona's desire to be immune to human love is based not only on an awareness of the uncommon nature and longing of the self, but also on an unresolved sense of love as both a gift and a lack. In "Cheated Elsie" this paradox is dramatized in the exchange between Elsie and the Fairies:

Elsie.
>Ah, what is this? Take back thy gift!
>I had not, and I knew no lack;
>Now I have, I lack for ever!.....
>Ah! why the present did I take,
>And knew not that a heart would ache?

Fairies.
>Ache! and is that all thy sorrow?—Beware, beware—a heart will break!
>
>(v. I, 218-219)

Set in easy rhymes, an overall flippant tone, and a fairy tale structure, the poem is supposed to teach a lesson—not too grave a lesson, but enough to convince one of the foolishness of possessing a heart. Out of this "worldly knowledge" the self-conscious persona projects a self-image foreshadowing the soul-weariness and exhaustion of spirit characteristic of the decadents. In "Insentience" the absence of love, which can be both a gift and a lack, makes the persona feel weary both physically and spiritually (v. I, 225). Such a condition is accompanied by a recurrent expression of self-inadequacy and guilt born out of the failure of the persona's dreams to love and to be loved. In "The Poppy" this sense of failure is equated to a physical falling and, as in "The Hound of Heaven," to the withering of his dreams:

> Love! *I* fall into the claws of Time:
> But lasts within a leaved rhyme
> All that the world of me esteems—
> My withered dreams, my withered dreams.
> (v. I, 9)

Alienated from the rest of humanity and nature, the persona is conscious of his solipsistic state, expressing the image of self as an "alien ghost" ("From the Night of Forebeing," v. II, 33). Failure to attain the highest ideal of love plunges the persona into the lowest depths, either of "love of basest rate" ("The Dread of Height," v. II, 19) or disgust with the physical aspect of love, the "horror of the/skin" ("Memorat Memoria," v. II, 216-17).

This self-recriminating persona's horror is closely linked to the fin de siècle obsession with the female figure as binary opposites: the ideal beloved depicted as the child-bride or the madonna, and the *femme fatale* or the fallen woman. Exemplifying the "cult of the child," Thompson's women figures range from the childlike beloved in "Daisy" and "The Poppy" to "The Making of Viola" and "To Olivia." The child-motif represents, as Honnïghausen identifies in *The Symbolist Tradition in English Literature*:

the pseudo-naive idyll of heaven...a kind of complement and counterweight to the desires and anxieties embodied in the *femme fatale*....The child bride—in this respect comparable to the hermaphrodite motif—symbolizes a love not endangered by its possible consummation. For this reason the poet is able to envision the Meynell's daughter as the incarnation of the "bodiless paramour" who, simultaneously present and distant, evokes the ambivalent state of love and sorrow informing poetry such as his own. (183)

Further, the "death of the child" motif, as in Thompson's poem "To Monica Thought Dying," anticipates the decadent poets' expression of "fusion of beauty and sadness" in the evanescence of life, symbolized in the deceased beloved (188). Reflective of "not only...male sexual inhibitions but also the more complex social and cultural disturbances of the period" (184), the late Romantic or fin de siècle "vision of woman" further emphasizes the split image of the female that is aestheticized in poets like Walter Pater, Lionel Johnson and Ernest Dowson.

The decadent image of the persona in Thompson's poems is that of a poseur—a self-conscious observer who exaggerates his own inadequacies into an aesthetics, a suave mannerist who finds his success in the fall itself. The pretentious and assumed elegance of the persona's language contrasts with the poet/Thompson's condition—as a possible alcoholic, a drug addict and even a suicidal. This contrast between the persona's mannerisms and echoes of the poet's frayed existence emphasizes the malaise of the turn of the century. In Hopkins, the deep sense of self-failure found an outlet through the analogy of Christ's life and his success through failure. Thompson made a similar attempt to find the recovery of self through the example of Christ's victory in failure, but often the attempt is too pat and hyperbolically expressed in phrases like "the slain hath the gain' and "scars of Thy conquest" ("The Veteran of Heaven," v. I, 149). The persona of Thompson's poems presents, at one level, the picture of self as loving but not loved, as an outcast, "Forlorn, and faint, and stark" enduring time's "barbed minutes" (36), as tempted through despair to self-destruction, "A dead fly in a dusty window crack" ("Manus Animam Pinxit," v. I, 83). For

Thompson failure was always imminent. In his life experiences and outcast existence, Francis Thompson's likeness to the decadents is obvious. In his study of Thompson, J.C.Reid emphasizes this aspect of Thompson:

> Although he did not know it, he was to become spiritually one of a band of young literary men, the "beat generation" of the late eighties and nineties, including Lionel Johnson, Ernest Dowson, Aubrey Beardsley, who were pursuing the decadent muse through the sinuous corridor of disordered lives. (36)

Terence Connolly, in his "Review-Article" on J.C.Reid's book, is outraged by what he refers to as Reid's "extravagant statements" and goes on to quote Holbrook Johnson according to whom Francis Thompson "cannot be located" in the "poetic impulse of the nineties" (204).[14] Without denying that Thompson's religious convictions were based on deeply felt principles, one can still trace in his poetic persona the beginnings of what was to develop into a more obviously self-parodying decadent aesthete. This link is an important one, for it highlights the crisis of the nineties as having begun in genuinely felt experiences. The extravagant indulgence on the artificial and the perverse as seen in the decadent personae is a later extension of the "experience of failure" into an "asthetics of failure." But it is true that, apart from his biographical affinity to the lives of other decadents, Thompson's poetry also foreshadows the decadent's major concerns. In rhetorical and stylistic treatment, Thompson's resemblance to the decadents is obvious. In the decadents we find Thompson's preoccupation with the montage of the self-conscious persona exaggerated to a pursuit of experience through the mannered posture of language and literary affectation.

Thompson's biographers and critics, however, have constantly taken care to mention Thompson's innocence, his lack of bitterness despite a tragic life, and his "strange other-worldliness" (Meynell, *Life* 249, 255). Alice Meynell had specifically pointed out Thompson's ability to laugh:

> He has been unwarily named with Blake as one of the unhappy poets. I will not say

he was ever so happy as Blake;—but few indeed, poets or others, have had a life so happy as Blake's, or a death so joyous; but I affirm of Francis Thompson that he had natural good spirits, and was more mirthful than many a man of cheerful, of social, or even of humorous reputation....It is pleasant to remember Francis Thompson's laugh, a laugh readier than a girl's, and it is impossible to remember him, with any real recall, and not to hear it in mind again. (331)

So also in his poetry, there are instances of intellectual and emotional assimilation when the decadent, quotidian self is renewed through the faith that transforms. Here, the uplift of the soul from the streets to the "red pavilion" of Christ's "heart" marks the tearing of the persona's mask. No longer an objective, analytical poseur, projecting himself as hard-hearted and immune to love, the persona in poems like "Arab Love Song," "A Fallen Yew," "Ad Amicam," and "Love's Varlet" openly responds to the lover, Christ's wooings of his heart, and is overcome by emotion, not mere sentiment. These responses, similar to the persona's reciprocated embraces of God, are marked by a discovery of the personal involvement in human and divine love as a deeply emotional one. This personal involvement entails the ability to integrate intellect and emotion so one can move from a state of detachment to empathy and finally to a state of equilibrium. In the man-God relationship this state, as pointed out before, is often culminated in the gesture of holding hands or the embrace which encloses the erring man and the loving God in a community of give and take. In Thompson's depiction of human love-relationships, this kind of equilibrium is very rarely reached. The persona-self, at the center of the human experience, is either too cautious or too naive. Despite Thompson's proportionate appeal to the merits of the body and the spirit, in the essay "Health and Holiness," one set of Thompson's love poems seems shy of exploring the depths of human passion or sexual love, and more comfortable to regard the "chaste and intelligential" (v. I, 83) aspect of human love. The beloved is perceived as "perfect," and her "body is a temple of God" (v. I, 100). She is also "Christ bearer," "Divine pavilion" and "A tenement for God and Peace" (*MHW*, 30). In the poem "The Bride of God and Thee," the Patmorean ideal of married love, in which the woman as queen is equal to man as king, is given expression to, "Yet she's thine equal..../That thou shalt rule her as her King,/And she shall rule thee as thy Queen" (*MHW*, 32). Ideal but also ethereal is the embrace between the man and the woman; it is an "aunthetic cestus of two girdling arms" (v. I, 37). In such a relationship, the persona declares, "Within your spirit's arms I stay me fast/Against the fell" (v. I, 82), "This soul which on your soul is laid,/As maid's breast against breast of maid" (v. I, 84), "What if no body she have for embracing?" (*MHW*, 27). In the other set of Thompson's poems of human love, there is a sense of guilt and frayed nerves at the rememberance of sexual love. In "A Narrow Vessel" and other poems, the persona regrets his "many wrongs":

> Thy softness (daring overmuch!)
> Profaned with my licensed touch
>
> (v. II, 81)

> Love, thou hast suffered many wrongs of mine,
>   When my sad youth, for hunger and lack of thee,
> Fouled, 0 most foul, its heavenly plumage fine,
>   Living on carrion.
>
> (*MHW*, 42)

> while I, chaste I,
>   In cheap immaculateness avert mine eye:—
>   Poor galley-slave of lust, rot in your gyve!"
>   This is her doom!
>
> (*MHW*, 43)

> My child! what was it that I sowed, that I so ill should reap?
> You have done this to me. And I, what I to you?—It lies with sleep.
>
> (v. II, 217)

Intellect and emotions are often fraught by a nightmarish clash between a need for stoic control and a neurotic desire for the passion of love. The shifts from images of freezing cold to burning heat illustrate a state of mind verging on madness:

> My thoughts, as weeds in waters are
> Congealed with severe frost
> *(MHW,* 19–20)

> I keep the lonely burning thought of thee
> Trimmed in my lonely heart
> *(MHW,* 25–26)

The erratic tone shifts from a reflective soliloquy to a rising pitch ending on a cry, to an ironic statement, echoing the persona's dissatisfied desire for love and companionship. This building up of diverse feelings and conflicting responses reveals accessible human feelings, whether disturbed, as in "I Love and Hate thee" *MHW,* 27) or more balanced, as in "Ultimum" (v. II, 102). The sane, rational, anti-Petrarchan stance of the persona is a surprising turn to the personality and fits in with the "enlightened" view he gains in his relationship with God: failure in human love may still imply success in divine love.

iii

Out of the pain, loss and disappointments of human love, the soul seeks, besides God, poetry as the avenue of consolation. In Thompson's vision, poetic creation is an expression of the soul's dependence on love and sanctity. In "Love in Dian's Lap" (v. I, 76), the female allegorical figure, Song, finds strength in the male allegorical figure, Love. However, in his attempts to express his faith and love in poetry, the poet suffers in his life. In "A Judgement in Heaven," Mary Magdalen reveals the Christ-like persona's "bloodied hairs," like "hairs of steel" his "torn flesh," and "the punctures round his hair." It is in his suffering that the poet gains Paradise, even as the "wounded" Christ gained victory ("The Veteran of Heaven," v. I, 149). In "The Mistress of Vision," this idea of success found in the apparent failure of a surviving artist is developed in a kind of choric message delivered by the mistress of vision:

> Pierce thy heart to find the key...
> Learn to dream when thou dost wake,
> Learn to wake when thou dost sleep
> Learn to water joy with tears,
> Learn from fears to vanquish fears.....
> Lose that the lost thou mayst receive
> Die, for none other way canst live.
> ("The Mistress of Vision," v. II, 8)

The poet transforms the quotidian world but what kind of world does he finally create? In early poetry, Thompson viewed the poet's world as the visionary realm of the miraculous, and poetry as a miracle. In this utopian paradise, dreams and poetry, like the magical drink, enlivens the world ("Love in Dian's Lap," v. I, 72). To escape the dark despair of the London streets the poet-persona creates his "Sinai-Seraphim" world. At first, this world is often conceived of as remote, abstract, and impalpable. The personal experience of self-sacrifice is objectified and made remote by the image from Romantic literary tradition, such as in "Ode to the Setting Sun" (v. I, 127).

It is in the *New Poems* that the poet's growth from the quotidian world into the world of "new things," achieved through self-effort and sacrifice, is expressed as synthesis of personal experience and scriptural prophecy:

> Thou makest all things new,
> Elias, when thou comest! Yea
> Makist straight the intelligential way
>   For God to pace into
> ("Carmen Genesis," v. II, 58)

Commenting on the poet as the "maker," Thompson notes, in his obscure fustian style:

> In the beginning, at the great mandate of light, the sea suddenly disglutted the earth: and still in the microcosm of the poetic, the *making* mind, Creation imitates her august and remembered origins. Still, at the luminous compulsion of the poet's intellect, from the subsidence of his fluctuant senses emerges the express and founded consistence of the poem; confessing, by manifold tokens, its twofold parentage, quickened with intellectual light, and freshened with the humidities of feeling....This is the function of the maker since God first imagined....For the poet is an Elias, that when he comes, makes all things new. It is a converse, alas, and lamentable truth that the false poet makes even new things old. (Meynell, *Life* 310)

Decrying what was to become the aesthetic tenet of the decadents, "Art for Art's sake," Thompson viewed poetry as an expression of reality, rather than of an abstraction, "She sees the Is beyond the Seems" ("The Singer Saith of his Song," v. II, 228). The condition of the poet's soul is "somewhat sweet" and "somewhat wan" till in the land of "Luthany" and "Elenore," the poet, "like a city under ocean," contains within himself "untumultous vortices of power" ("Contemplation," v. II, 13). This power comes from his possession of vision and reality—the heavens and the streets.

Out of the city of earthquakes, out of "perished cities" glutted with "cold houses," (v. II, 115) "and towns" of "copied fragments" (v. II, 181), the poet builds his own new empire, imparting "the grandeurs of his Babylonian heart" (v. II, 181), even as the self discovers its renewed relationship with God in the enclave of his shaded arms. Thompson's expressions of man's experience of failure in worldly and other-worldly relationships appear as breaks in human-human or human-divine communication. The poet-persona often finds his experience of failure reflected in the moments of poetic unproductiveness. Often the responses to these moments of failure have to be gleaned from a plethora of poems experimenting with diction, rhythm, and imagery, and poems reflecting literary and scriptural influences. But the responses are organic to the growth of the poetic mind and the struggling persona. They reveal a faith in God-man relationship similar to Hopkins'.[15] But Thompson's persona also experiences a faith burdened with the soul-weariness and unresolved frustrations which were to become part of the characteristic mood of the nineties and which Thompson could foresee:

> I know her for I am of the age, and the age is hers. Alas for the nineteenth century, with so much pleasure, and so little joy; so much learning, and so little wisdom; so much effort, and so little fruition; so many philosophers, and such little philosophy; so many seers, and such little vision; so many prophets, and such little foresight....the one divine thing left to us is Sadness. Even our virtues take their stamp; the intimacy of our loves is born of despair; our very gentleness to our children is because we know how short their time. "Eat," we say, "Eat, drink, and be merry; for tomorrow ye are men."
>
> ("Moestitiae Encomium," v. III, 111)

In *Between Heaven and Charing Cross: The Life of Francis Thompson*, Brigid M. Boardman refers to the complexity of Thompson's vision of faith and cynicism as "the twist of paradox...shaping, or misshaping all human life, the slender but unbreakable link between its tragedy and comedy" (301).[16] This complexity is reflected, as Boardman reveals, in his apparently simple public poems, the Odes written "between the Jubilee of 1897 and the peace treaty with South Africa in 1902" (302). These Odes were commissioned by William Lewis Hind, the editor of the *Academy*, a journal for which Thompson wrote regular reviews and articles. In these Odes (such as "To England," "Ode on the Death of Cecil Rhodes," and "Nineteenth Century"), emerge Thompson's concerns for Western warfare in the colonies and fears regarding the Empire's "over-confidence" which resulted in the failure at the Boer War:

> Thompson was not alone in seeing the Boer War as the present warning of long term repercussions. Yet the expectations for the future which were stimulated by the new century were still mainly directed to an age of future prosperity due to the discoveries bequeathed to it by one just past. For Thompson, its coinciding with the

> War brought a revival of his concern for warfare, shorn now of much of the glamour and appeal the battle once held for him. He saw the greed giving rise to the ravages in South Africa spreading out to infect the whole of Western civilization 'till the awful war comes in which the European nations will finally explode their feuds, their treacheries, the jealousies—and ultimately themselves. (302)

Thompson depended on the *Academy* and its commissioned Odes for survival. However, cynicism and bitterness, born out of a "homeless" existence on the streets of a nation that held a "rich estate" in Africa and Asia through colonialism, marked his Odes. The patriotic rhetoric of "honour" and "blood" is underlined by a grim reminder that "It ("rich estate") is not thine to barter, thine to let it rot" (qtd. in Boardman, 302). However, Thompson, while criticizing British expansionism, did not censure its political, economic or cultural exploitation of the colonized. His critique expresses the blend of varying response to early and mid-Victorian imperialism and that of the later era. Patrick Brantlinger in *Rule of Darkness: British Literature and Imperialism 1830-1914* discusses the continuities and variations in the expression of ideology in early and late Victorian literary writing.[17] In the "Ode on the Death of Cecil Rhodes," the fusion of rhetoric (Rhodes as "Visioner of visions") and reality ("So large his dream, so little come to act") emphasizes the "twist of paradox" in human history. Boardman notes the symbolism inherent in the poem, "At the end, the isolated grave on the Matappo hilltop becomes a symbol for the failure of the high ideals and the loneliness the failure must bring" (304). Shorn of the rhetoric, these poems express Thompson's "fear for the nation's future" (305) as well as his insight into the historical ambiguities of the successes and failures of the nineteenth century.

Notes

1. John Walsh, *Strange Harp, Strange Harmony: The Life of Francis Thompson* (New York: Hawthorn, 1967) 216.

2. Wilfrid Meynell, ed., *FrancisThompson: Poems and Essays*, three volumes in one (Freeport, N.Y.: Books for Libraries Press, 1947).
   Note: All subsequent quotes from Thomson's poems and essays refer to the above text unless otherwise specified.

3. John Evangelish Walsh, ed., *The Letters of Francis Thompson* (New York: Hawthorn, 1969) 31.

4. Everard Meynell, *The Life of Francis Thompson* (London: Burns and Oates, 1913) 8.

5. J.C.Reid, *Francis Thompson: Man and Poet* (London: Routledge and Kegan Paul, 1959) 107.

6. Terence L. Connolly, S.J., ed., *Poems and Plays by Francis Thompson* (New York: Doubleday and Co. 1957) 55.
   Note: References to poems from the above source will be indicated in the chapter as *MHW,* followed by page numbers.

7. W.H.Gardner and N.H.MacKenzie, eds., *The Poems of Gerard Manley Hopkins* (Oxford: Oxford UP, 1967) 57.
   Note: References to poems from the above source will be indicated in the chapter as *PGMH*, followed by page numbers.

8. Terence L. Connolly, S.J., ed., *Poems of Francis Thompson* (New York: Appleton-Century-Crofts, 1941) 399.

9. Norman H. MacKenzie, *A Reader's Guide to Gerard Manley Hopkins* (Ithaca, New York: Cornell UP, 1981) 157.

10. Gardner and MacKenzie, eds., 283.
    Note: In the notes the editors point to the "nature of Mary" as "the softening, humanizing medium of God's glory." Hopkins' poem dwells on this human aspect--the relationship between Mary and the persona's self.

11 St. Augustine, *The Confessions of St. Augustine*, transl. by J.G.Pilkington (Norwalk, Conn: The Heritage Press, 1963), 47-48.

12 Louise M. Rosenblatt, *The Reader, the Text, the Poem: TheTransactional Theory of the Literary Work* (Carbondale: Southern Illinois UP, 1978) 27.

13 George G. Williams, "Thompson's 'Grace of the Way'," *The Explicator* 9:2 (1950): 16-17.

14 Terence L. Connolly, S.J., "Laudanum or Poetry?" *Renascence*, XIII (Summer 1961): 204.

15 Francis Thompson, "The Preferential Anthology," *Minor Poets: Criticism Newly Discovered and Collected*, ed. Terence L. Connolly (Los Angeles: Anderson and Ritchie, 1949) 70.
Note: Thompson had developed his faith independently but it is illuminating to note that he had read at least one of Hopkins' poems, that is, "Heaven Haven," as is evidenced in his review, "The Preferential Anthology," first published in *Academy*, July 19, 1902.

16 Boardman, Brigid M. *Between Heaven and Charing Cross: The Life of Francis Thompson* (New Haven: Yale UP, 1988) 301.

17 Patrick Brantlinger. *Rule of Darkness: Britich Literature and Imperialism, 1830-1914* (Ithaca: Cornell University Press, 1988) 8-9.

Chapter 4

Lionel Johnson and the Aesthetics of Failure in Fin de Siècle

Against the backdrop of an "age of tedious woe,/that snaps and snarls," Lionel Johnson etched out a life true to a tradition and to "the private fictions of order":

> Thine was a life of tragic shade;
> A life, of care and sorrow made:
> But nought could make thine heart afraid,
> Gentle *Saint Charles!*[1]

The assumption that one can "make" one's life and shape it to a desired rather than a given form underlines the decadent generation's philosophy and "aesthetics of failure":

> The primary vision of the poets of Johnson's generation involves an aesthetics of failure: a consistent self-distance; a consciousness of failure which is the necessary prelude to the tragic vision of Yeats's later work. In general, the aesthetics of failure was formulated in revolt against the Victorian moral order. Sickness became an ironized honesty in a social world that proclaimed health while manifesting generalized sickness.[2]

Commenting on Johnson, W. B. Yeats pointed out, "it often seemed as if he played at life, as if it were an elaborate ritual that would soon be over. I am certain...that he was himself that mystic and cavalier who sang: 'Go from me: I am one of those who fall....'"[3] Johnson created a self which adopted a Celtic and a Catholic tradition in life and a classical tradition in art. He often played the role of the Epicurean decadent, who in Pater's *The Renaissance* tradition could escape into his own "mind and spirit":

> When the endless region of faith and doubt is once entered, life becomes weary of itself: and to remain without that land, contented with the colours of a rainbow and a curtain, the sound of a storm and a sonata, appears the higher, more dignified way.[4]

Then there is the committed critic in *The Art of Thomas Hardy*. Here the Samuel Johnson persona was an "image of what he wished to become and, at the same, an image almost absurdly antithetical to what he was"; it represented "not only an anti-self but a figure symbolically opposed both to what Johnson saw as "Decadent excesses and to a part of himself he wished to disown"[5]:

> For men of wide culture, able to range at ease through the literatures, the histories, the sciences of long gone times, danger lies upon the side of vague and dreamy thought, in which nothing, not truth itself, is at a stay.[6]

There is also the hieratic spiritualist—the persona who looks towards the "other world":

> I will be a priest of the Church of England as I have so often dreamed of being. I have one monotone to which I will intone my life: "I will be a priest": not, you may think, the music of the spheres: but at least not out of tune.[7]

The persona in Johnson's poetry often shifts from one role to the other. Our understanding of the "mask" and the anti-mask" in poetry has been greatly enriched by W. B. Yeats' theories and their application in his poetry. However, Lionel Johnson, Yeats' close friend and associate in the Celtic movement, developed through the voice of his persona the mask and anti-mask of the decadent hero—the isolated, melancholy escapist, the committed eighteenth century Johnsonian figure with a desire for certitude, and the transcendentalist with a longing for philosophical idealism, fellowship and love, extending to a Whitman-like acceptance and celebration of life and death. This Yeatsian opposition of the persona's dual self, however, is not a consciously developed theory in Johnson's poetics; it is rather reflective of Johnson's own divided pull toward and away from the decadent aesthetics. Barbara Charlesworth in *The Dark Passages* points out the "personal quality" in Lionel Johnson's short story "Incurable" (which appeared in *The Pageant*, I, 1896):

> On the surface the sketch pokes fun at aestheticism by describing a young poet who feels that life holds no more for him. He decides to commit suicide, regretting only that the river most convenient for his purpose is waterlily-less. But even without waterlilies he finds it possible to imagine himself floating down, like a male Lady of Shalott (in Elizabethan costume), to a heartless and unthinking London. In the midst of this reverie he falls absent-mindedly into the river, comes to himself, and swims strongly for shore.
> Underneath its satire, the story has a personal quality, a note of both self-mockery and self-pity.[8]

The pull away from decadence is dogmatically presented as a rejection of decadence through the assumed persona of Samuel Johnson in *The Art of Thomas Hardy*:

> It is a sick and haggard literature, this literature of throbbing nerves and of subtle sensations; a literature, in which clearness is lost in mists, that cloud the brain; and simplicity is exchanged for fantastic ingenuities. Emotions become entangled with the consciousness of them: and after-thoughts or impressions, laboured analysis or facile presentation usurp the place of that older workmanship, which followed nature under the guidance of art. (2-3)

But as Linda Dowling points out, the persona's dogmatic exterior is underlined by the typically decadent desire for escape from the present:

> For all its angry rejection of Decadent sensibility, Johnson's book nevertheless shares in it—not simply because a tortured ambivalence is a characteristic Decadent attitude, but because *The Art of Thomas Hardy* is concerned with its narrator's attempt to escape from himself and his time into art. Disturbed by the subversion of a rich and spacious and significant past, by an incoherent trivializing present, Lionel Johnson saw in aesthetic terms Pater's epistemological problem of "each mind keeping as a solitary prisoner its own dream of a world." Imprisoned in the

solipsistic present, a writer could yet reach the world of the past by becoming at once a character in it and a commentator upon it." (292)

Decadent aesthetics emerges out of a complex and often conflicting politics of race and nationality of late nineteenth century British imperialism and colonialism. While exposing the politics, it often succumbs to its ideological prescriptions. The aesthetes thus are often caught at the juncture of expressing or not expressing the anomalies of their society; they often choose to silence the expression of their epistemological problem in the idiom of art. Yet, in the very formal texture and shaping of their art, the aesthetes reveal the peculiar form of oppositionality and binarism that operates in the larger socio-political framework of late nineteenth century Britain. In Johnson's poetry, this dialectic is often encountered in terms of a divisiveness that defies synthesis. Even as his poetry reflects the tensions of his socio-political milieu, it also wrenches itself from its contextual base to comment upon it.

As Johnson's pull toward and away from decadent aesthetics was often erratic, there are personae in his poetry who fall between the "mask" and the "anti-mask," personae whose attachment to life collides with a desire for the after-life. The ambiguity of the intermediary persona can be sensed as one reads the poem "Victory." The reiteration of the color "white," such as "white steps," "white roses," "white upon the shadowy lawn she stood," set against the background of "the dark and visionary wood" brings into focus the two concerns of the persona: life and death. In his "Notes on Walter Pater," Johnson observes the connotations the word "white" held for Pater:

> The Welsh word for *white* means also something which is a combination of *holy, reverend*, felicitous; much in the sense of Herrick's White Island. In the finer portions of Mr. Pater's work, there is a "whiteness," a "candour" indescribably felt, through this purity and cleanliness of it, as though there were "a sort of moral purity" in art of so scrupulous and dainty a distinction.[9]

At another point in the essay, Johnson points out the association of spiritualism with white as reflected in Pater:

> Things hieratic, ascetic, appealed always to him. Dissolute and lawless art, flung upon the world in a tumultuous profusion and disorder, was not art in his eyes. His favourite type of "hero" was le bel serieux, self-contained, of an almost monastic habit, with the "white soul" of youthful Virgil, yet sensitive to everything fine in life. (29)

In this connection, Ian Fletcher points out Pater's influence on Johnson's generation:

> Pater was devoted to the word 'white': Marius's old home "White-Nights," the "white light" and the mystery of so-called "white things" are three examples of that 'sacred' colour. His sense of the word was transmitted to his followers of the 1890s. (293)

Seen as an extension of the Paterian symbolism, "white" in Johnson's "Victory" could reflect the purity of life:

> Down the white steps, into the night, she came; Wearing white roses, lit by the full moon (162)

But the color "white," in Johnson's poem "Glories," is also associated with "death's perfection" as in Dante Gabriel Rossetti's "The Blessed Damozel":

> No Alban whiteness doth she wear,
> But death's perfection of that hue (35)

Thus, "white" in Johnson's poem is an idealistic conception of both life and death, and appears as the feminine figure, "she." However, in the context of late nineteenth century expansionist Britain, "white" and "dark" as opposing categories of valuation extended to explain, theorize and ultimately institutionalize the racial hierarchies used to justify British colonialism as well. Moreover, the curious interplay of "shadowy lawn" and "visionary wood" underscores symbolic, perhaps orientalist, notions of "civilized" English gardens versus the "wild" mysterious jungles of the tropics. Exoticized by the Romantic "idealism," these distant lands become objects of possession, both by colonial policy makers as well as artists and writers. For purposes of articulating the overwhelming fear of losing the past in the encroaching reality of present industrialization and machinization, and fear of death itself, both for the person and the nation, the decadent aesthete plays with symbols which evoke both an antiquated return to the past and a disruption of historical movements through creating anti-Romantic ideals of artifice.

The final effect of the poem is orchestrated on the visible movement of the poem: from outside ("into the night, she came") to inside ("And went into the room..."); from the natural "night" and "day" to "a room of burning lights." The poem reflects in some measure Johnson's constant pull toward and away from the decadent aesthetics. The poem suggests (in the first two stanzas and the beginning of the third) the shift in the persona's attachment to philosophical ideologies—from romanticism and naturalism to decadence—expressed in Johnson's concern with the central decadent rejection of nature in favor of artificiality. In *The Decadent Imagination*, Jean Pierrot discusses this seminal characteristic of decadent aesthetics:

> The rejection of nature...was to become even more intense during the decadent period. Indeed, one of the specific features of the decadent esthetic is a conscious determination to diverge as far as possible from nature, in an overt repudiation of the classical dogma that the aim for all art is the imitation of nature. For the decadent, art is identified with the artificial, and it is the artificial that must be developed by every available means.[10]

The movement in the poem "Victory" is further corroborated by the dedication of the poem to George Moore. Moore's *A Mere Incident*, in particular, was greatly influenced by the French Decadent Huysman's *A*

Rebours, which expresses a "rejection of nature" in the "form of an antiromantic depreciation of the so-called beauties of natural landscapes" (166).

Now, in Johnson's poem "Victory," the persona's "white she" moves not only away from the night "lit by the full moon" to the "room of burning lights" but also from a waiting "lover" to a "loveless husband" sleeping "his brute sleep." This information in the last stanza of the poem pulls the reader to a closer examination of the issues involved. Until the last five lines of the poem, the movement from naturalism or even romanticism ("visionary woods") reflects the philosophical bent of the persona. It is in the last five lines that the persona's attitude to his own philosophical attachment is revealed. The value words, "loveless," "brute," "comfortless" and the image of the colorless "ashen flame" placed against the "dark" "woods," gather to emphasize the persona's self-distance and self-parody in accepting decadence as his dominant philosophical ideology. The break in the final refrain "She turned not back," while implying a certitude reached, also ironically suggests the persona's awareness of his own blindness. Ian Fletcher, in his notes to the poem, suggests, "The breaking of the refrain in the last two lines enacts the "victory" (325). But it is not a simple victory, even as the persona of the poem is not a simple self. The "victory" implies, ironically, both success and failure. This ambivalence in the attitude of the persona and in the inevitable responses of the reader is crucial to understanding Lionel Johnson's constant preoccupations with antithetical elements, such as art and religion, life and death, and success and failure, as they are played out against the backdrop of British nationalist as well as colonialist discourses.

Gerald Kent Clifton, in his doctoral dissertation titled *'Lost in Light': A Study of Lionel Johnson's Poetry*, expanded on the polarity of religion and art in Johnson's use of the "central pattern of imagery," light ("of Neoplatonic mysticism and...Newman's Catholicism") and darkness ("associated with his desire to write poetry").[11] Johnson develops other polarities through a recurrent pattern of images which creates a picture true to the decadent assumptions of life as conflict:

> I have passed over the rough sea,
> And over the white harbour bar . . .
> ("In Falmouth Harbour," 8)

> Dark Angel, with thine aching lust
> To rid the world of penitence:
> Malicious Angel, who still dost
> My soul such subtile violence!
> ("The Dark Angel," 52)

> But now in vehement disarray
>   Go time and thought,
>   Distraught
> With passion kindled at thy ray.
> ("A Proselyte," 83)

"Born into life, busy with life" (223), the persona lives out the decadent spirit of world-weariness, "A life of noise": "Our wearier spirit faints,/Vexed in the world's employ" (12). Like Thompson's persona buffeted by the London streets, Johnson's persona is weary of the city life and seeks an escape from its noise and, paradoxically, its death-like silence, from "the turmoil of the town," "the sullen gloom, the faces full of care," "Thoughts of the world, unkind and weary," the "sudden gloom that invests this city strange," (13-14), "the sleeping town" (8). The persona seeks to escape not only the place which has become an exile for him, but also the present time: "Weary, the cares, the jars,/The lets, of every day" (10). Even as Thompson's persona dwelt on the innocence and freshness of childhood, so Johnson's persona is nostalgic for "childhood's delicate memory" which is one way to undo the "sad, destroying work" of "hard, dull hours" (37). Quoting from Johnson's "A Dream of Youth," Barbara Charlesworth, in *Dark Passages*, clarifies how memory of past is also a grieving of one's lost youth: "The mourning of youth and its recollection as a period without struggle, without consciousness of self within or responsibility without, is a major theme in Johnson's poems" (94). Memory also revives the past with its "ancient grace" in the midst of present despair. In "Oxford," the persona, through memory, revives the wondrous city of the past:

> City of weathered cloister and worn court;
> Gray city of strong towers and clustering spires
> ....
> Where at each coign of every antique street,
> A memory hath taken root in stone...
> That is the Oxford, strong to charm us yet:
> Eternal in her beauty and her past.
> (115)

The poem exemplifies the central tenet of Aestheticism. The movement, as discussed by Leon Chai in *Aestheticism: The Religion of Art in Post-Romantic Literature* is centered on

> a desire to redefine the relation of art to life, to impart to life itself the form of a work of art and thereby to raise it to a higher level of existence....The history of Aestheticism, then, is in effect the history of a quest for specific impressions or experiences that are felt to possess an intrinsic significance—above all, the experience of beauty and the experience of form....Thus meaning becomes identified with intensity of impression. But if the meaning of an impression lies in its intensity, an impression can only be meaningful in a transitory sense at best. Hence the incessant quest for new sensations and impressions, and, ultimately, the failure of that quest. What results from this failure is not a renunciation of experience as meaningful but an attempt to discern a transcendent element within it.[12]

Analyzing Proust's *A la recherche du temps perdu*, Chai illustrates how recollection of various past moments of the "narrator's existence which transcends time" provides a means of re-experiencing "the moment as consisting of an emotion" (x, xi) and recovering "each moment of his tacit, their tacit formation of an ideal sequence. Thus he perceives his whole life as composing implicitly a work of art" (xi). The "emphasis on form" results "also from the recapitulation of certain themes (life as drama, life as music) arising from the Aesthetic quest" (xiii). In this context, Johnson's poem "Oxford," through the evocation of artist's works, celebrates life as architecture. The line "A memory hath taken root in stone" rings with Ruskin's theory of the symbolic expressiveness of architectural edifices. In "The Seven Lamps of Architecture" from *Stones of Venice*, Ruskin observes:

> Thus age itself becomes the consecration of an edifice—not however, merely an account of that edifice's silent testimony to the passage of time but because it becomes for us the visible embodiment of all the emotions it has witnessed. In this respect it becomes symbolically expressive. Through it we experience the consciousness of a past epoch or moment....What remains is the consciousness of emotion itself as an affirmation of life. In the process, emotion assumes a sacred quality. As a feeling of the presence of something sacred, this consciousness of emotion corresponds to the experience of seeing natural objects symbolize a divine presence. Thus human edifices offer ultimately a secular form of sacred symbolism.[13]

In Johnson's "Winchester," memory has the power to transform the present, "the shadowy world":

> Our thought of thee is as the thought
>   of dawn, when nights are bitter:
> The shadowy world begins to glitter;
>   ....
> A place of friends! a place of books!
>   A place of good things olden!
> With these delights, the years were golden
>   And life wore sunny looks.
>   They fled at last:
>   But to that past
>   Am I in all beholden.
>   (177-178)

The persona images the failure of life, both in time and place (at the present moment and in the city), in three striking ways—as living in a dark prison, as a fall, and as ageing or withering of life. A persistent image is that of the persona caught in the dark, in the mist or in a narrow space—a prison: "You wait upon my heart, my heart a tomb," "this close world" (23), "Only the mists, only the weeping clouds:/Dimness, and airy shrouds" (25), "the melancholy vale" (84), "the dark way" (110), culminating in the image of life as a "tragic shade" (121); the persona, racked by misery, guilt and despair must "shudder in the shade" (111) and meditate upon "the shadowy nature of the world" (147). In "Quesque Suos Manes" the central idea of "to each man his own appropriate suffering," referring to the "Pythagorean doctrine of reincarnation" as expounded by Aeneas' father (translation by Ian Fletcher), brings to the fore the vision of man suffering his punishment as a shade:

> We each suffer our own punishment as a shade. Then are we sent out through wide Elysium and possess the fields, a scanty band. (Clifton 332)

Another image for the failure of life is the fall. The concern with self's fall and rise in Hopkins carried, as noted in chapter two, a sense of man's struggle with the physical and the spiritual; in Francis Thompson it implied the struggle between the quotidian and the miraculous. In Lionel Johnson the same image recurs and is somehow bound up with the legend of Johnson's own death:

> "Much falling"...alludes to Johnson's constant physical as well as his moral falls, from hansoms, down stairs and the final falling on sleep in the Green Dragon Public House....There is the famous phrase quoted by Arnold in his *Study of Celtic Literature*: "they went forth to the battle, but they always fell," so Johnson taking pleasure in his doom: "in ten years I shall be penniless and shabby, and borrow half-crowns from friends" and knowing that "The end is set:/though the end be not yet". (lxvii-lxviii)

In the poem, "Mystic and Cavalier," the persona caught between the "shadowy depths" and the "pure skies" expresses self's dilemma in the image of a fall:

> Go from me: I am one of those, who fall
> What! hath no cold wind swept your heart at all, In my sad company? (24)

While the horsemen, active in the battle, "fall on sleep" and achieve sudden calm, the persona looks forward merely "to fall" with a despairing hope that his "spirit may have sleep." In another poem, "A Cornish Night," the empty circularity of repeated falls is echoed by the persona in the voice of Iseult mourning for her dead lover, Tristan:

> Tarry to pour some balm upon mine head,
> Some pity for a woman, who hath wed
> With weariness and loneliness, from fall
> To fall, from bitter snows to maybloom red:
> The hayfields hear, the cornlands hear, my call!
> From weariness toward weariness I tread;
> And hunger for the end: the end of all. (24)

The landscapes and the settings themselves reflect the persona's inner fall: "night falls," "and the world as well/Was darkened over us, when that night fell!" (16), "Look, where the embers fade, from ruddy gold/Into gray ashes falling without bruit!" (19), "The fires of hearth are fallen" (20), "our fires are fallen from their blossoming height,/And linger in sad embers" (21), "there broods/Thunder, thunder; and rain will fall" (33), "Age long to watch the falling day,/And silvery sea, and silvery moon" (87). In "Ireland," through the voice of the captain battling for Ireland, the persona links the image of fall with the possibility of actual defeat and hope for ressurrected success (94). Supplicating the "King of Souls," the repentant persona, in "The Darkness," seeks deliverance from life's dark shadows and fears:

> Now give me light! I cannot always walk
> Surely beneath the full and starless night
> Lighten me, fallen down, I know not where,
> Save, to the shadows and the fear of death. (125)

The third dominant image of the failure of life is that of an apocalyptic end. One of the decadent preoccupations was the "carpe diem" philosophy intensified by a belief in the annihilation of the individual and civilization. In *The Decadent Imagination*, Jean Pierrot traces some of the motive forces governing the decadent pessimism flowing through French literature and finally evident in English decadent literature as well:

> The underlying melancholy of the decadent era stemmed first and foremost from a pseudomedical theme, that of the degeneration of the race....This belief had its origin in Darwinian theories concerning the evolution of species: like all animal species, man must follow the same path as that of each individual organism, from youth, through maturity, to old age. The peoples of Europe, inheritors of centuries of evolution, were therefore threatened with inevitable senility, and their civilization doomed to imminent death....Hovering over this entire era, therefore, we find the myth of a Twilight of the West, of a wholesale destruction of civilization....
>
> At the individual rather than the collective level, the idea then gaining ground was that modern man lives in a constant state of imbalance summed up in the new term neurosis; since the human machine was now worn out, man could keep going only by living on his nerves. (46-48)

This apocalyptic fear of the inevitable end of the Western civilization also paralleled and anticipated, by 1897, the Diamond Jubilee of Queen Victoria as well as the various threats to the imperial sovereignty of Britain: the Boer War in South Africa, the rise of Irish Republican Brotherhood and Indian nationalism, the Jamaican demand for accession to the United States, "sedition" accompanying Buddhist revivals in Ceylon (Sri Lanka), resentment of "educated Africans of Sierra Leone and the Gold Coast" toward the "anglicization of the senior Civil Service."[14]

For the fin de siècle artists and writers the end of their world is linked to an end of their exoticist project, a project emerging from a need to experience new sensations through exploring "alternative horizons," as Chris Bongie clarifies in *Exotic Memories: Literature, Colonialism and the Fin de Siècle*. For the purposes of this study, exoticism is defined as a nineteenth century literary and existential practice that posited another space, the space of an Other, outside or beyond the confines of a "civilization"....What modernity is in the process of obliterating "here" might still prove a present possibility in this alternative geo-political space: such is the primary credo of the exoticist project. The initial optimism of this project, however, gives way in the second half of the century to a deep pessimism stemming from the rapid spread of colonial and technological power. How can one recuperate "elsewhere" what civilization is in the process of eliminating if this same process has already taken on global proportions?[15]

Analyzing the "methodological presuppositions" and the "historical trajectory" of exoticism, Bongie engages in the "redeployment" of some "exoticist (and, by implication, metaphysical) categories of thought—such as modernity/tradition, civilization/savagery, Same/Other, presence/absence" (5-6). In the context of historical change, "narratives of loss" invoke "value" as "a theoretical object of concern." Frederick Jameson, in *The Political Unconscious*, using Max Weber's notion of "rationalization" as a "mediatory code" in the formation of social institutions, argues that in pre-capitalistic societies of "the traditional village" and "tribal culture," each activity is "symbolically unique, so that the level of abstraction upon which they could be compared with one another is never attained."[16] It is only in the post-French Revolution period and the spread of the "market system" which led to "secularization of life under capitalism and the breaking up (or, in the current euphemism, the 'modernization') of the older tradition-oriented systems of castes and inherited professions," that, as Jameson points out, "the relative value of these activities can begin to be thought." Jameson emphasizes the "binary, means/ends logic" that underlies the "rationalization" process of "drawing all activities and institutions together onto a single plain of equivalence and thereby erasing whatever qualitative differences might once have distinguished them" (Bongie 7). This logic of binarism underpins the "nostalgic reconstruction" and "utopic projection" of the notion of value (Bongie 7).

Bongie further explores the two central concerns of the "exoticist project": "'authentic experience' and 'sovereign individuality'" (9). Approaching the project as a "transnational phenomenon," Bongie argues, "This absorbing concern with, and fundamental grounding in, the future-oriented time of secular history, which characterizes modernity, is the common thread joining all forms of nineteenth-century exoticism" (15). He also highlights the contentious temporal and spatial sites that the exoticist project locates itself in:

> As a project, exoticism necessarily presumes that, at some point in the future, what has been lost will be attained "elsewhere," in a realm of ad-venture that bypasses the sort of contemporary present that a symbolic form such as the bildungsroman, by contrast, prepares us for. But if exoticism partakes of modernity and its promise, what the future promises—and here, of course, is the central irony of this particular project—is a recovery of the past and of all that a triumphant modernity has effaced. Indeed, the very emergence of this project is unthinkable without such a triumph. Because of this vicious circle that draws the future and the past together, the exoticist project is, from its very beginnings, short-circuited: it can never keep its promise....Since, as I have argued, exoticism is an essentially posthumous project and thus precluded from ever truly realizing what it sets out to achieve....the fin de siècle writers...were forced to confront openly what earlier writers could more easily ignore: namely, the end of the exotic—that end which from the beginning haunts it and which, toward the close of the nineteenth century, would become ever more glaringly apparent. (15-17)

Elaine Showalter, in *Sexual Anarchy*, describes the fin de siècle as a period of "cultural insecurity," based on fears of "degeneration and collapse" of European history, race and civilization at the very height of imperialism:

> The 1880s were a turbulent decade in English history. The making of vast industrial fortunes was balanced by the organization of trade unions and the founding of the British Labour party. Imperialist adventure in Africa, where diamonds were discovered in the Transvaal in 1880, occurred while urban poverty and homelessness in England received dramatic attention. Hopes for the Empire were undermined by acts of political terrorism committed by anarchists and Irish nationalists. Even while

the age of imperialism was at its height, there were also fears of degeneration and collapse. England was often compared to decadent Greece and Rome, and there were parallel fears of the rise of captive peoples.[17]

Referring to the influence of late Victorian science, Eugenics and "the new science of physical anthropology," Showalter concludes that the fear of the Empire being "undermined by racial degeneration" legitimized "racial differentiation and hierarchy" (5). Thus "racial boundaries" were "among the most important lines of demarcation of English society" (5). Moreover, there "was a major crisis in class relations...The theory of urban degeneration furthermore held that poverty led to a general deterioration of the race" (5).

From Hopkins and Thompson to the decadent era there is a growing preoccupation with ageing, sickness, nervous depression and suicide. Hopkins recorded his sense of failure often as a kind of fatigue, a weariness with life: "And I do not know how it is, I have no disease, but I am always tired, always jaded, though work is not heavy, and the impulse to do anything fails me or has in it no continuance (Abbott, ed. *Letters* 190). In another letter to Bridges, Hopkins had dwelt on the tragic suicide attempt by a young man in their community (282). Francis Thompson (whose suicide attempt Wilfrid Blunt has mentioned in *My Diaries*) also expressed a sense of nervous strain in his letter to Wilfrid Meynell: "The fact is my nerves want taking up like an Atlantic cable, and recasing. I am sometimes like a dispossessed hermit-crab, looking about everywhere for a new shell, and quivering at every touch. Figuratively speaking, if I prick my finger I seem to feel it with my whole body."[18] Thompson lived out the paradox of childlike youthfulness and old age; Johnson too was both young-looking and haggard, as described by his friends, contemporaries and acquaintances. George Santayana in *The Middle Span* looks at the way Johnson appeared to his friends--haggard and persecuted:

He still looked very young, though he was thirty, but pale, haggard, and trembling. He stood by the fireplace, with a tall glass of whisky and soda at his elbow, and talked wildly of persecution....As he spoke, he quivered with excitement, hatred, and imagined terrors.[19]

Richard Le Gallienne's portrait, in *The Romantic 90's*, however, emphasizes Lionel Johnson's youthful appearance:

I looked with wonder at the young scholar, who, it proved, was but a year younger than myself, being twenty-three. Not an advanced age, indeed, but not even the knowledge that he was Lionel Johnson could make him look more than fifteen, and he never seemed to look older as long as he lived, which was only two years longer than his friend Dowson, for he died when he was but thirty-five. His little, almost tiny, figure, was so frail that it reminded one of that old Greek philosopher who was so light of weight that he filled his pockets with stones for fear the wind might blow him away.[20]

The dominant impression of Johnson among other contemporaries was that of the decadent poseur, wearied by sickness and the burden of life, and verging on self-destruction. Ian Fletcher notes:

We hear of him from Stopford Brooke. "Lionel Johnson and Miss O'Brien dined with us. Miss O'Brien is gay and fresh. L. Johnson is mournful and decaying. Both are young, but Johnson is also very old. A small, dark, withered man...." [evidence of Stopford Brooke, Ms. Journal, 4 June 1898]. A photograph taken at this time agrees with this description; it shows what can only be described as a haunted face....It is from the latter part of 1899 that we date his final physical decline. On that small delicate body the repeated doses of spirits were, at last, taking full effect....There is something of an epic quality about this single-minded self-destruction. (vii)

Besides alcoholism, another of Johnson's specifically decadent preoccupations was with suicide, as reflected in the persona of the young poet in his short story "Incurable."[21] In one of his letters to Richard Le Gallienne, he mentions a suicide attempt by his brother, revealing how close he was to a whole generation on the brink of self-destruction: "But if ever you had a brother committing ineffectual suicide, and driving an invalid mother to the verge of the grave, you would understand my troubles of that day."[22]

The persona of the aged man, warning others of the brevity of life, the passing of time and the loneliness of old age was not only the decadent mask worn by Johnson in life, but also a recurring figure in his poetry. The persona, through a consciously self-pitying stance, often becomes the mouthpiece for expressing the evident failure of life:

> Pity thyself! youth flies, youth flies.
> Thou comest to the desert plain,
> Where no dreams follow in thy train:
> They leave thee at the pleasaunce close;
> Lonely the haggard pathway goes.
>   ("Lines to a Lady," 37)

> Their dignity of perfect youth
> Compels devotion, as doth truth:
> So right seems all, they do, they are.
> Old age looks wistful, from afar,
> To watch their beauty, as they go,
> Radiant and free, in ordered row;
> And fairer, in the watching, grow.
>   ("A Dream of Youth," 43)

> Ah how the fire of youth is fair, Yet may not be forever young! (45)

The full force of "the tragic shade" within which we mortals live is felt starkly in the poem "In a Workhouse." The persona is a young man observing the old in a workhouse. In the earlier persona of the old man, Johnson could only warn the youth; but now, in the voice of the young man, he can express the stark reality, the horror and the bleakness of all life ending in old age and senility:

> Old hopes I saw there: and perchance I saw
> Other old passions in their trembling age,

> Withered and desolate, but not yet dead:
> And I had rather seen an house of death,
> Than those live men, unmanned, wasted, forlorn;
> Looking towards death out of their empty lives.
>
> (147)

Inhabitants of "the shadowy nature of the world," the old have lost their dreams, their faith, and their "impassioned trust." Their tragedy is not glorious like that of the Greek heroes. This realization comes as a blow to the young decadent whose pose of world-weariness, on the one hand, becomes a reality. On the other hand, his search for keen sensations and vivid dreams becomes a mockery when he can foresee his own old age in the workhouse:

> Nor wisdom of bright dreaming came there back
> To these dulled minds, that never had the time,
> The hard day's labour done, to do with dreams.
> Naught theirs, but sullen waiting for no end
> ....
> These were none else, than worn and haggard things,
> Nor men, nor brutes, nor shades: and yet alive.
>
> (147)

Against such a scenario, the persona in Lionel Johnson's poems takes two antithetical positions—that of a participant in the aesthetics of failure and that of a theorist responding to the aesthetics with philosophical idealism and Catholic mysticism. From the latter standpoint the persona projects certain ideals as alternatives to the failure of life—fellowship, love, death and eternity.

The decadents developed a growing fellowship, often considered "unnatural", among themselves. Whether expressed as homosexuality or not, the bond among the male individuals became a saving grace from the interminable solipsism into which their age and decadent aesthetics plunged them. The ideal of male fellowship was largely disseminated to the decadents through the ideals of Walter Pater. In *Marius the Epicurean* the sustaining bond of friendship with Flavian is Marius' escape from absolute loneliness:

> And, dating from the time of his first coming to school, a great friendship had grown up for him, in that life of so few attachments—the pure and disinterested friendship of schoolmates. He had seen Flavian for the first time the day on which he had come to Pisa.... Marius knew that those proud glances made kindly note of him for a moment, and felt something like friendship at first sight.[23]

In Volume II of *Marius the Epicurean*, Pater dwelt on the extension of one-to-one friendship to a feeling of general "brotherhood":

> There is that in death which certainly makes indifferent persons anxious to forget the dead: to put them—those aliens—away out of their thoughts altogether, as soon as may be. Conversely, in the deep isolation of spirit which was now creeping upon Marius, the faces of these people, casually visible, took a strange hold on his affections; the feeling of human kinship, asserting itself most strongly when it was about to be severed for ever. (217)

Some of the letters of Lionel Johnson to his friend Charles Sayle sound very much like the younger Marius:

> I have been intensely interested in life in many ways—and my philosophy, or systematic want of it, has received its final perfection in the few days lately lived at Oxford. Not the beautiful spell and associations—not the thought and the idea of the holy and eternal city—rather the personal delight and fascination of contact with true life and true love: the sense of fellowship has seized hold upon me. By nature unfamiliar enough and unemotional, still the close intimacy of those I can feel for in common has been a dreamy revelation of happiness. (Russell, ed. 72)

In another letter to Charles Sayle, dated 29 June, 1884, Johnson writes:

> It seems so altogether strange, all this unconventional friendship of strangers, and the something higher than friendship crowning our friendship. I can imagine no more beautiful happiness than to walk with you by the sea in the winter and the cold

fresh breath of wind and waves (167)

Elaine Showalter, in *Sexual Anarchy*, points out the impact of emerging feminism on late nineteenth century male psyche: "While one response to female power was an exaggerated horror of its castrating potential, another response was the intensified valorization of male power, and expressions of anxiety about waning virility" (10). One outcome of this valorization is the creation of male bonding in response to "the new feminist order": "A significant aspect of the construction of masculinity was the institution of "Clubland," the network of men's clubs which served all social classes and provided alternatives and substitutes for domestic life. Clubland reinforced the spatial as well as the social boundaries separating men and women" (11). The emergence of the Rhymer's Club can be seen as an artistic gathering of males that served some of the same psychological needs for construction and preservation of masculinity. Moreover, as Showalter further explains, "Fin de Siècle Clubland existed on the fragile borderline that separated male bonding from homosexuality and that distinguished manly misogyny from disgusting homoeroticism" (13). In the legal sphere, "the Criminal Law Amendment Act of 1885...made all male homosexual acts, private or public, illegal....This was the law under which Oscar Wilde would be convicted and sentenced to two years of hard labor at Reading Gaol" (14).

In *Dark Passages*, Barbara Charlesworth traces biographical details that highlight Johnson's detachment from family, his rejection of Anglicanism, the family form of worship, and the movement of his search of the transcendental from "Buddhism into Shelleyan Platonism, Emersonian Transcendentalism, Whitmanesque Humanism" (84). Through his conversion to Roman Catholicism, Johnson seemed to have achieved "an aristocracy of culture," "intellectual superiority and wideness of culture" (88-90). In England, Catholicism was associated with peasants (mainly the Irish immigrants) or the aristocrats. As Charlesworth explains, "Both of these groups were free in Johnson's mind from any connection with

Philistia—and indeed, his discovery of Irish ancestry was, in Santayana's opinion, another of Johnson's ways of rejecting the Philistine world" (89). Moreover, Johnson connected the Catholic Church with an "outmoded dignity." Charlesworth concludes, "Thus Johnson's acceptance of the Catholic faith, however genuine it may have been, did not really serve as a bond between him and the rest of the world; on the contrary, he made his religion into yet another protective wall" (90).

As a counter-point to his own isolation from society, Johnson projected in his poetry a persona who seeks male bonding. In his poetry, the ideal of friendship is constructed as the persona's responses to the failure of life. Moving out of the city of gloom and defeat, the persona in "De Amicitia" seeks the White City, "Land of the Love, that never fails" (104-5). The adulation of friendship reaches a crescendo in the repeated addresses. While everything else declines, the persona holds on to "friendship's confederacy" as one way out of the despair and inconstancy of life (105-106). Moreover, the persona seeks the companionship of his friends to defy the fear of death:

> Poor powerless Sorrow! Helpless Death!
> Think they to worst me in the end?
> Come when they will, my Faith still saith:
> I face them with a single friend.
> ("Friends," 134)

In "To Alfred Ferrand," the persona envying the several lives (roles) an actor lives claims a friend as his relief from monotony and loneliness:

> Yet sometimes, for a little space,
> Pitying my loneliness, they send
> To give my days a little grace,
> The goodliest of their gifts, a friend.
> (211)

The persona celebrates Winchester as a place where he claims:

> A place of friends! a place of books! (177)

> Friends fail me not; but kindlier
> Can no friend be, than thou hast been.
> ("In Memory of M.B.," 34)

A significant recurring pattern is that friends are the way to "celestial communings" ("Friends," 135) and eternity. Johnson's persona displays an Emersonian exuberance in poems that celebrate this belief:

> I thank Eternal God, that you are mine,
> Who are His too: courageous and divine
> Must friendship be, through this great grace of
>   God;
> And have Eternity for period.
> ("To Certain Friends," 80)

Through fond memory, the living can bring their dead friends back to life. Occasionally, women are included among this ideal fellowship:

> For men and women, safe from death,
> Creatures thine, our perfect friends:
> Filled with imperishable breath,
> Give thee back life, that never ends.
> ("Bronte," 70)

However, it is male friendship that dominates and evokes various levels at which this bonding is realized: philosophical, literary and spiritual. In "Plato in London," "The Classics," "Winchester" and "The Ballade of the Caxton Head," books and their male authors are the persona's companions in times of loneliness. Substituting books for human friends, the persona encloses himself within the aesthete's desired realm of *objects d'art*. The persona in "Plato in London" distillates the culture of the past from a world of "noise and glare" (7). He relates himself to Plato on a host-guest level. In contrast to the persona's "world of noise and cold," Plato's home is in the "city of high things." While communing with Plato, the persona is in a state of "impassioned contemplation" and of intense aliveness so acutely described by Pater as burning "always with this hard, gemlike flame."[24] In "The Classics," the persona lists Virgil, Sophocles, Aeschylus, Horace, Lucretius, Plato, Thucydides, and Pindar, among others, as his companions. In this connection, Thornton in *The Decadent Dilemma* refers to Johnson's cultivation of an "artifice of eternity":

> In a poem that familiarly and rather charmingly goes through a roll-call of "The Classics," the authors are much more than the names on dead books; they become the companions, the "friends that fail not" among—one presumes—many failing friends....What one usually means by Classical reference, the myths and the legends of the ancient world, is on the whole absent from Johnson's poems. He longed to join literary and classical fraternity and, by cutting himself off from contemporaries and living among books as he did he began to construct his own "artifice of eternity."[25]

In the jaunty voice of a paper-boy or a salesman, the persona in "Ballade of the Caxton Head" proclaims the value of books:

> Let moralists talk of the lifelong friend:
>   But books are the safest of friends, say I!
>   (210)

Johnson's own advice to his friend, Francis Russell, runs in the following lines:

> Read Whitman: he will never fail you, that is the test of divinity: Jesus and Shelley and Whitman, they are stedfast in faith, never wavering. Men think that the Whitman doctrine is a mean unwholesome poison trying to pass for the breath of God. (Russell, ed. 203)

Out of a conviction of the degeneration of the human race, the growing senility and final destruction of civilization, grew the Ninety's skeptical cynicism toward sexual love. Hardy's poems, perhaps the most enduring depictions of man-woman relationships, prefigure the end-of-the-century despair at the corrosion of love, the tragic moments that scar human bonds. Towards the latter part of the nineteenth century, a definite attitude toward sexual love was developing, from avoidance of such issues (as in Hopkins) to an idealization of the man-woman relationship (as in Patmore and Thompson), and finally to a cult of male friendship among the decadents, including homosexuality. The late nineteenth century English poetry confronts the barrenness of man-woman love relationships. Pierrot examines how, even before Freud, the theory of the unconscious, as disseminated through von Hartmann's *Philosophy of the Unconscious*, was far-reaching:

> Hartmann's unconscious has a biological dimension as well as a psychological one; it is that force or energy that obliges individuals to conform with the higher ends of the species, even despite themselves, as when they are controlled by their instinctual mechanisms, for example....As far as the influence is concerned, however, Hartmann did clearly assert that the unconscious plays a determining role in our sexuality. Convinced, like Schopenhauer before him, that sexual activity is in itself obscene and ridiculous, and that man would never subject himself to it unless some unknown and unconscious force were obliging him to bow to the superior desire of the species to ensure its perpetuation, he denounced love as a purely subjective illusion serving to mask the essential mechanism of reproduction. (Pierrot 120)

One of the outcomes of such an outlook, an artificial reduction of woman as contemptible, as natural and not spiritual, is seen in Schopenhauer and Baudelaire particularly. Schopenhauer reduced love to "nothing other than the specialized instinct."[26] Greatly influenced by the current German and French philosophical and literary trends, as well as by a growing sense of pessimism, the English decadents reacted to a loss of faith in "natural" love by a theory of "antinaturalism": "Antinaturalism leads quite naturally to antifeminism, since woman symbolizes nature" (Pierrot 124).

In the process of defining "decadence," Elaine Showalter elaborates:

> Decadence is a notoriously difficult term to define. In one sense, it was the pejorative label applied by the bourgeoisie to everything that seemed unnatural, artificial, and perverse, from Art Nouveau to homosexuality, a sickness with symptoms associated with cultural degeneration and decay. In another sense, it was a post-Darwinian aesthetic movement that crossed European boundaries. The decadent aesthete held that nature was "an unfeeling and pitiless mechanism"; religion, a "nostalgic memory"; and love, a biological instinct for perpetuating the species....The decadent aesthete rejected all that was natural and biological in favor of the inner life of art, artifice sensation, and imagination....women were seen as closer to "Nature," to the body, and to a crude materialism, while men were aligned with "Art," to the intellect, and to spiritualism. The most brutal and influential version of this misogyny came from Baudelaire, who described woman as a being entirely governed by her biological and physical impulses: "Woman is the opposite of the dandy. Therefore she inspires horror..." The debasement of women's bodies, standard in much French Decadent writing, reached a degree of extraordinary disgust and loathing in Huysmans's *Against Nature*. Women reappear as objects of value in decadent writing only when they are desexualized through maternity or thoroughly aestheticized, stylized, and turned into icons or fetishes. (169-170)

Showalter further quotes Fraser Harrison who suggested in *The Yellow Book* that threatened by feminist emancipation the decadents turned to "homosexuality, prostitution, addiction to alcohol and opiates, sterile relationships with children, and in some cases, forlorn celibacy" (170). As "refugees fleeing in the face of bewildering social evolutions," they were "either cared for by sisters, intimidated by New Women, or like [Lionel] Johnson, after 'four or five glasses of wine,' denying that 'a gelded man lost anything of intellectual power'" (171).

Ironically avoiding the bleak cynicism of a pure decadent, Lionel Johnson posits the theory of male fellowship, of a generalized brotherhood in place of man-woman love: "So the universal of happiness would be the absolute equality of act and word by the pervading uniter, Love" (Russell, ed. 128); "I want corporate love" (130). He further elaborates in other letters:

> Love—love towards one, one alone, one in the world; what is this but love for all,

if you think rightly? When a yearning stirs within the spirit to become one with a high lonely star, to make two one, that unity may be the sole existence, then love of men and women is sprung to light out of dark hesitation; the single love is the myriad love—isn't it so? (148)

But the spirit of love is in all and transmutes clay into air and stars—the clay and dust of daily ugliness and commonplace Love; don't you know the meaning of universal love the passion which is only reason and the mind of God, so unintelligible and infinite? (162)

The Johnson persona's euphoric celebration of male fellowship reconciles a decadent detachment from man-woman love with an overriding involvement in the political brotherhood of the Irish National Movement and a truly Catholic spiritual desire for Christ's love. From the mask of the disillusioned decadent arises the anti-mask—the transcendentalist committed to the Irish cause, to peace, human fellowship and divine love. In the poem "Friends," the intense love felt by the persona, among his friends, teaches him the eternity of God's love:

> But in the eyes of every friend,
> Voice, or the holding of his hand,
> I learn, how love can never end:
> Oh, Heart of God! I understand.
> (134)

In the poem "Our Lady of France," through prayer and dream the persona subdues "Thoughts of the world, unkind and weary" to celebrate Christ's crowning of "Laborious day with love" (13). In "A Descant Upon the Litany of Loretto," the persona's invocation to Mary is rich in allusions to mystical love:

> Ah mother! whom with many names we name,
> By lore of love, which in our earthly tongue
> Is all too poor, though rich love's heart of
> flame (109)

In the second part of "Carols" the quick exchange of dialogue among friends reflects their shared fellowship and a faith in the brotherly love that resides in their eternal home (130).

The persona in "Magic" dissociates himself from "logicians" and finds an alternative to his present existence (described as "the ground, where shadows are") in the ritual of the magician. His dilemma is to make the final break from the engirdling solipsism to reach eternal love.

Very similar to Francis Thompson's persona is the Johnson persona's rejection of cerebration for feelings. Johnson's poem "Sursum Corda," dedicated to Thompson, illustrates a faith in the emotions as against the intellect:

> Lift up your hearts! We lift
>   Them up
> To God, and to God's gift,
>   The Passion Cup. (145-146)

In "Poems from the Henn Ms.," the persona affirms the heart with love which triumphs over the coldness of life. In contrast to the "cold air," "the gray-walled/city," "cold sunlight," "cold hills," "cold waters," and cold days of "wind chills and wails," "grey shadowed skies" where "all sunlight struggling fails" lies "the city not made with hands,/Where Love makes merry for new hearts won" (252). On the other hand, the persona, earth-drawn, selects the life on earth where brotherly love is possible (252).

Out of this celebration of male fellowship, culminating in divine love, the persona projects the after-life as an answer to the present sorrow:

> I would, that with eternal wings we went,
> All sorrow spent, all things
> Ended, save the song love sings!
>   ("To Morfydd Dead," 124)

Therefore, the persona seeks death and consciously pursues it. Although the voices in "Vigils" warn, "Death ends life: And life is death" (64), and he himself knows that "Death and the shadows tarry not" ("The End," 173), the persona regards death as a desired relief from life. "In Falmouth Harbour," death is imaged as a "calm harbour" lying below "Long, terraced lines of circling light" (7). In contrast to the turmoil and the noise of life, "seas of desolate storm," death is a place of "pure rest" where there is "deep peace," "No sight, no sound, no living stir/But such as perfect the still bay" (7, 8), where "Memories of open wind convey/Peace to this harbour strand" (8), perceived in another poem as a place where the traveller can rest from the "labour of life" (33). The persona conceives of death as a land of dreams, "Death's dreamland" ("In Falmouth Harbour," 8), "death means dreaming" ("Gwynedd," 20), "dreamland, deathland" ("Bells," 89).

The equation of death with dream often gave the decadents an excuse to indulge in acts of self-destruction through alcohol, drugs, or suicide. Besides an outlet for the decadent impulses, desire for death was perceived as the ultimate spiritual objective in practically all the religious, philosophical and political systems Johnson dabbled in—Buddhism, Emersonian Transcendentalism, Catholicism, Celticism, and Irish Nationalism. In all these belief-systems and movements, death is viewed as perfecting life. This outlook, in Johnson, took the dual-form of a decadent obsession with refinement and an idealistic conception of death as the way to eternity. In "By the Statue of King Charles at Charing Cross," the dead king attains a dignity lacking in life:

Vanquished in life, his death
By beauty made amends:
The passing of his breath
Won his defeated ends.

Brief life and hapless? Nay:
Through death, life grew sublime.(11)

In the seventh of the "Poems From the Henn Ms.," the persona realizes that the fruition of life is in death:

> Find its supreme fruition here, where the hours
> Fall past to death and death's control
> Faint oracles are fair in passionate flowers?
> (249)

In "The Silent," the persona, living the "lone life beneath/Sad skies," entreats his dead friends to sing to him. However, though he is drawn to death, his position is not clear. Alive, he fears death and this clash of impulses is evident in the poem: "shadowy spheres," "fellowship of gloom," "Chill pathway of the tomb" (158-159). In the poem "Nihilism," the persona counters with a fear of life, not death: "of life I am afraid" (160).

The reader, dealing with Johnson's often vague and generalized language, must realize that the epithets "gray" and "gloom" in Johnson's poetry gain meaning according to the context. In themselves, they are neutral, with the potential to connote either negative or positive responses. For example, in one poem London is described as "*O gray, 0 gloomy skies!* what then?/Here is a marvellous world of men" (117); in other poems, the persona dwells on the "grave eyes gray" of the three-year-old child (36), accepts "this world of the gray cottage by the hill" (21), and celebrates rain which falls "through eve and gentle gloom" (21). In "Morning Twilight," the scene and the persona's mood are described through the images of darkness, gloom and light (254).

As noted by Gerald Clifton in *Lost in Light*, "To Johnson, language is always an inferior imitation of the object or concept it attempts to describe, a 'false' diminution of universal truth....and the best way to express such truths in language was to name objects according to their general qualities" (94). These generalizations often leave the reader with an impression of repetition, vagueness and even of contradiction. Although there is no evidence that Johnson was consciously using the reversibility of language to reflect the antithetical nature of his concepts, it does achieve this effect. Death is imaged as a "larger room" (23), as a "home" (14), "a sleeping city" (84), the "sacred darkness" (68); but so is a state of deathlessness (again an ambiguous term, here meaning a negative state of spiritual barrenness) in the poem "Visions." Deathlessness, in this context, is described as a "mighty house of hate" and "utter black." Death and deathlessness imply inner states, perhaps states of mind. Johnson often images death as dark, as a "gray land" that has not touched "white brows" (45); but he also images death as white, as in the previously quoted poem "Glories" (35). So, it is context alone which determines whether the epithets carry a negative or a positive connotation. It is this generalized use of language that demands a greater attention from the reader towards even the tiniest of details. This situation is further complicated by the fact that the persona's attitude toward death is often reflected in opposing though equally compelling images. While it is, on one hand, a desired city, death is also a comfortless "room of burning lights" (162). Sometimes death is seen as "kindly" ("Oracles," 73). At other times, it is a fearful, dark, cold end to life ("Darkness," 125). Sometimes death is a rest; at other times an antagonist, a challenge to the persona:

> The impotence of death is plain to us,
> Whose faith victorious
>   Laughs death into defeat
>   ("Vita Venturi Saeculi," 229)

> We challenge death beyond denial
> Against the host of death we make our trial.
>   ("The Coming of War," 39-40)

>   May death not be by youth defied?
>   ("A Dream of Youth," 44)

> Where now is death? where that grey land?
>   (45)
> We give our life, our heart, our breath,

> That you may live to conquer death
> ("Our Lady of the Snows," 76)

In "Friends," the dualism regarding death is clarified to a certain extent. It is the persona who can qualify death as he wills. If faced alone, death can be the "imperious Powers"; if faced with a friend it is but a "Poor powerless Sorrow! Helpless Death!" (134). Moreover, love and fellowship can conquer death.

> Death cannot conquer all: your love and mine
> Lives, deathlessly divine. ("Brothers," 221)

Similarly, in "The Sleep of Will," the "long, and thin, and white" fingers of the "unfathomable sleep" imply the touch of death. It is the will of the persona which can strengthen the will of death: "Your will were mightier than before,/Made one with mine" (160).

Thus, for Johnson's persona, both life and death can imply either a positive or a negative stage of human existence, suggested by the phrases "death in life," and "life in death" (170). As seen above, images like "gray," "gloom," "white" and "dark" can refer to either life on earth or to death, and either to a sad or a happy state. One other striking and central image, implying life or death, is that of the "shade" or the "shadow." While life was seen as a "tragic shade" (121) and a reflection of "the shadowy nature of the world," death too is often referred to as a shade/shadow. In "A Dream," the ambiguity of "shade" and "fainter shade" can be seen to echo the ambiguity of separating life from death, or death from life (111). In "The Darkness," the self supplicates the master of spirits to uplift him from the "shadows and the fear of death" (125). In "Hugo," the persona laments the loss of Victor Hugo (139). In "The End," the persona echoes the 'carpe diem' philosophy in the line: "Death and the shadows tarry not" (173). In "To the Saints," the erring persona appeals to the "white souls" of the saints:

> Oh, let it not be malice, that thus brings
> My soul within the shadow of death's wings!
> (223)

Even as living in "the tragic shade" implied a failure of life, so the shade or shadow of death implies a failure of death as an idealistic conception:

> What choice is ours, but tears? For the world fails
> I
> Have mourned, because all beauty fails, and goes
> Quickly away: and the whole world must die.
> (148)

Associated with fall, death is opposed to life: "Here rise and fall, here live and die" (117). Elsewhere life too was perceived as a fall:

> Some pity for a woman, who hath wed
> With weariness and loneliness, from fall
> To fall, from bitter snows to maybloom red
> ("A Cornish Night," 24)

The conviction that what Johnson's persona is struggling to express is the meeting place between the opposing elements, the borderline between the mask and the anti-mask, where concepts are interchangeable, is clearly stated in lines such as "You saw there death in life; you will see life in death." So, if death implies fall, in Johnson's poetry, it also implies a rise:

> This only can be said:
> He loved us all; is dead;
>   May rise again.
>   ("A Burden of Easter Vigil," 10)

If it implies the clash of swords, "swords of death rang round my way" (123), it also is "gracious" and "kindly"— "the last music": "Holy my queen lies in the arms of death:/Music moves over her still face" (42). Similarly, if life implies the jarring noise of the city streets, it also rings with the "pleasant village noise" that "Breaks the still air" ("In England," 29). If life is a "haggard pathway" (37), it is also blessed with the "memories," "splendours," and the "desires" of the earth (20). In "Gwynedd," the persona's celebration of life involves anti-decadent, Whitman-like acceptance of all its aspects:

> We will not wander from this land; we will
> Be wise together, and accept our world:
> This world of the grey cottage by the hill,
> This gorge, this lusty air, this loneliness:
> The calm of drifting clouds (21)

Even the image of life as a fall is transformed:

> The wet earth breathes ancient fair fragrance forth;
> And dying gales hang in the branches, blow
> And fall, and blow again: our widest home
> Is with rich winds of west, loud winds of North,
> Sweeping beneath a gray and vasty dome
>   ....rich rain
> falls on our hearts
> (21)

Johnson's aesthetics become relevant in the context of the politics of late nineteenth century British Imperialist ideology of "Manicheanism," a dualistic philosophy which served the British Imperialist project by assigning opposing values to the worlds of the colonizer and the colonized. Frantz Fanon in *Black Skins, White Masks* and *The Wretched of the Earth* delineates the characteristics of the colonial world in terms of its Manicheanism:

> The colonial world is a Mainichean world. It is not enough for the settler to delimit physically, that is to say with the help of the army and the police force, the place of

the native. As if to show the totalitarian character of colonial exploitation the settler paints the native as a sort of quintessence of evil....The native is declared insensible to ethics; he represents not only the absence of values, but also the negation of values. He is, let us dare admit, the enemy of values, and in this sense he is the absolute evil.[27]

Abdul JanMahomed in *Manichean Aesthetics* clarifies the two-way process of "social pathology" and psychological "dependency" created by colonization.[28] While the decadents seemed to withdraw from the world of politics, their aesthetics of "art for art's sake" was no doubt shaped by the prevailing world-view. Barbara Charlesworth's observation further substantiates my argument:

> Johnson brooded not on sanctity but on sin. His poetry is much more concerned with damnation than with beatitude....Very often God seems remote to Johnson, or if He be near, He comes in vengeance not in love...."The Dark Angel" tries to reach a better and more hopeful solution, yet again most of the poem is taken up with terrible internal conflict of which the resolution is simply imposed by a change from Manichean to Neoplatonic theology." (91)

The most striking response to the imposed dual reality occurs in the synthesizing image of life and death. The persona's response to the image of life and death as "tragic shade" is a projection of past historical "hero" figures who embody the ideal of victory in defeat as against the present realities. Some of these figures are Newman, King Charles I, Lucretius, Charles Lamb, and Victor Hugo, culminating finally in the vision of Christ. A curiously consistent feature in the persona's presentation of the historical figures is his highly personal and subjective evaluation of them as masters of their destiny in a world alien to heroism. These figures are etched, as it were by an artist, against the background of grey skies, "Sombre and rich" (11), of "thunders of shaken dark" (57), against "a life of tragic shade" (121) and "terrible thunders/hurled/From out night's battling clouds" (138). These sketches, thus, are subjectively created configurations of life-death and triumph-failure antitheses in a world of dialectical opposition.

However, the persona is never satisfied with seeing them as mere dualities.

In "Falmouth Harbour," the persona paints an allegorical picture of Newman as a Catholic soldier fighting with "Death." The very motif of warfare is fraught with the questions that are the persona's central concern--how does one transform failure into success or how does one discover success in failure:

> Hence by stern thoughts and strong winds borne,
> Voyaged, with faith that could not fail,
> Who cried: *Lead, kindly Light!*....
> ...Fighting with Death in Sicily (8)

As in early Hopkins and Thompson, the rhetorical use of warfare in Johnson's poetry underscores a masculinist aesthetic in the practice of religion and politics in late nineteenth century Britain.[29] Armored with faith, Newman's courage is seen to lie in his own acceptance and transformation of earthly sorrow to "songs and prayers":

> The freedom of the living dead;
> The service of a living pain:
> He chose between them, bowed his head,
> And counted sorrow, gain (9)

In "By the Statue of King Charles," the persona's subject is not just the historical King Charles I, but his statue—an artistic emblem, which implies the transformation of life-form, wraught with "passionate tragedy," into an art-form, a "sweet austerity." The persona can stand back and reflect on the artifact. His contemplation appears as a passive act, but is underlined by an active deliberation, thus paralleling the apparent antithesis of failure and success:

> Brief life, and hapless? Nay:
> Through death, life grew sublime....
> He triumphs now, the dead,

Beholding London's gloom. (11-12)

In "Lucretius," the persona portrays a figure of death-in-life, with "worn and haunted eyes." It is through death that Lucretius gains the wisdom which truly makes him "King of men":

Thou knowest now, that life and death
Are wondrous intervals:
The fortunes of a fitful breath,
Within the flaming walls. (57)

Charles Lamb is the persona's projection of the decadent's self-division. He with his "merry-meaning looks" is opposed to the decadent torpor and failing spirit (121). And yet like Lionel Johnson, and the Johnson persona, Lamb lived in the "age of tedious woe,/That snaps and snarls!" The "tragic shade" echoes the "tragic generation" of the decadents with whom the persona self-consciously identifies himself. For the persona who already has shown a need for an authority figure, Charles Lamb becomes a source of instruction:

Gentle *Saint Charles!* I turn to thee,
Tender and true: thou teachest me
To take with joy, what joys there be,
And bear the rest. (121)

The stoical figure, "walking thy London day by day," is quaintly reminiscent of other figures who either influenced the decadents or participated, consciously or unconsciously, in their moods and aesthetics. Two such figures who stand out are Thomas De Quincey and Francis Thompson; both are often portrayed as exiles on the streets of London. Thompson has also been constantly described as gentle and sweet natured, despite his tragic misfortunes. So is Charles Lamb by Johnson's persona. Johnson was not merely using Lamb in place of Thompson; rather, Lamb embodied for him what Thompson did not—"The brave heart" which could calmly accept "life's pain" and make "life's turmoil sweet."

This juxtaposition of Lamb and Thompson gains weight when we bring to the poem what we know about Johnson's opinion regarding Thompson. Johnson, as a critic, admired Francis Thompson. In "The Soul of Sacred Poetry," collected in the *Post Liminium* essays, Johnson points out the positive elements in Thompson and other sacred poets:

> so poets, from the young Jesuit martyr Southwell to Mr. Thompson, have played with a devout audacity upon the theme of the Divine Passion. Not shirking the truth, out of a falsely reverent reticence, they stir the imagination to mystical journeyings in heavenly places, by their Franciscan fearlessness and cunning (Whittemore, ed. 113-114)

His own poems on Catholic themes show the influence of Thompson, Crashaw and Patmore. But Johnson also saw the negative effects of Thompson's influence, as his note to Katherine Tynan reveals:

> He has done more to harm the English language than the worst American newspapers....He has the opulent, prodigal manner of the seventeenth century; a profusion of great imagery, sometimes excessive and false.... Incapable of prettiness and pettiness: for good and bad, always vehement and burning and—to use a despised word—sublime. *Sublime*, rather than *noble*! too fevered to be austere: a note of ardent suffering, not of endurance.[30]

Paradoxically, Johnson could identify with as well as dissociate himself from Thompson. In Johnson's poems, Charles Lamb, a figure from the past serves as a much more approachable example of the success-in-failure hero than does Thompson or any other contemporary. Johnson's persona thus exposes the self's psychological attempts to objectify its own inner division. Passively receptive to the wisdom of an older male literary figure, the distant *"Saint Charles,"* he constructs a relatively simple mode of resolving inner conflicts.

A similar simplification of deeper significance by an obvious punning on the name "Victor" occurs in the poem "Hugo." The persona's exaggerated sentiments are focused on the paradox of victory achieved through peace, not war:

> Victor and loving Lord, who, seeing this poor world
> Wasted and worn with wrongs, wouldst not war, but
>   peace,
> And little children's laughter, and the law of love!
>   (138)

As prototypes functioning within the culturally rich medium of art and religion, the historical figures represent not their historically verifiable natures but the misty area of mythical transposition of self into the figure of Christ. Perhaps nowhere is the conflict of opposing elements and selves better resolved than in the compelling image of Christ as "Victor Victim":

> Would, that with you I were imparadised,
> White Angel around Christ!
> That, by the borders of the eternal sea
> Singing, I too might be:
> Where dewy green the palm trees on the strand,
> Your gentle shelter, stand:
> Where reigns the Victor Victim and His Eyes
> control eternities!
>   ("De Profundis," 150)

The lines from "Dominica in Palmis," translated by Ian Fletcher read: "The passion of Christ is sung: Jesus! who redeemed us, Victor dead on the Cross" (327). In the poem, "Hawker of Morwenstow," the Catholic-convert friend's eyes "closed in death" but opened on "the Victim's Breast" (169). It is in the death of Christ that the opposition of success and failure is resolved:

> Yea, thorny crown
> And purple robe and rods beating the face,
> And death of God: I spoke not to displace

> The glory of that passion....
>
> It were so fair to win;
> So fair to die therein?
>
> ("Poems From the Henn Ms.," 247)

Again and again, from the human to the Christ figures, the persona grasps a pattern that is useful for his own final discovery of man and Christ as both creators and exemplars of masculine spiritual beauty that is harmony. It is from perceiving the central paradox of Christ as "Victor Victim" that we, as readers, can attempt to understand what appear at first as strikingly conflicting images of life and death, victory and defeat. A significant concern of Johnson's persona, throughout the gamut of his experiences, is to seek order out of chaos, fellowship out of isolation, success out of failure. Lord Francis Russell in his autobiography commented on Johnson's spiritual quest:

> He (Johnson) taught me a lesson I have never forgotten, and that is all the supposedly real things of, that is to say the external things, the physical things, the humours, the happenings, disgraces, successes, failures are in themselves the merest phantoms and illusions, and that the only realities are within one's own mind and spirit.[31]

Johnson's quotation from Walt Whitman, at the beginning of the poem "Sir Walter Raleigh in the Tower," reflects the eternal search of the persona-self:

> I do not know what you are for (I do not know
> what I am
> for myself, nor what anything is for),
> But I will search carefully for it even in being foiled,
> In defeat, poverty, imprisonment--for they too are great. Did we think victory great?
> So it is—but now it seems to me, when it cannot be helped, that defeat is great.
> And that death and dismay are great.
>
> --Walt Whitman (240)

Notes

1. Lionel Johnson, *The Collected Poems of Lionel Johnson*, ed. Ian Fletcher (New York: Garland, 1982, rev. ed.) 121, xvii.
   Note: All subsequent quotes from Johnson's poems refer to the above text and will be indicated by page numbers in parenthesis.

2. Ian Fletcher, ed. "Introduction," *The Collected Poems of Lionel Johnson* (New York: Garland, 1982, rev. ed.) xvi.

3. W. B. Yeats and Lionel Johnson, *Poetry and Ireland* (Churchtown, Dundrum: Cuala Press, 1908) 19-20.

4. Sir Francis Russell, ed., *Some Winchester Letters of Lionel Johnson* (London: George Allen and Unwin Ltd., 1919) 183.

5. Linda C. Dowling, "Pursuing Antithesis: Lionel Johnson on Hardy," *English Language Notes* 12.4 (June 1975): 289, 290.

6. Lionel Johnson, *The Art of Thomas Hardy* (London: Elkin Mathews, 1894) 162.

7. Russell, ed., 85, 133.

8. Barbara Charlesworth, *Dark Passages: The Decadent Consciousness in Victorian Literature* (Madison: University of Wisconsin Press, 1965) 82.

9. Thomas Whittemore, ed., *Post Liminium: Essays and Critical Papers by Lionel Johnson* (London: Elkin Mathews, 1911) 40.

10. Jean Pierrot, *The Decadent Imagination 1880-1900*, trans. by Derek Coltman (Chicago: The University of Chicago Press, 1981) 166.

11. Gerald Kent Clifton, *'Lost in Light': A Study of Lionel Johnson's Poetry*, Diss. (University of California, Irvine 1978) ix.

12. Leon Chai, *Aestheticism: The Religion of Art in Post-Romantic Literature* (New York: Columbia University Press, 1990) ix, xi.

13 John Ruskin, "The Stones of Venice," *Works* 8 (London: G. Allen, 1903) 233-234.

14 James Morris, *Pax Britannica: The Climax of an Empire* (New York: Harcourt, Brace, and World, 1968) 484-489.

15 Chris Bongie, *Exotic Memories: Literature, Colonialism and the Fin de Siècle* (Stanford: Stanford University Press, 1991) 17.

16 Frederick Jameson, *The Political Unconscious: Narrative as a Socially Symbolic Act* (New York: Cornell University Press, 1981)

17 Elaine Showalter, *Sexual Anarchy: Gender and Culture at the Fin de Siècle* (New York: Viking, 1990) 4.

18 Wilfrid Scawan Blunt, *My Diaries: Being a Personal Narrative of Events, 1888-1914*, Part I (New York: A. A. Knopf, 1921) 147; John Evangelist Walsh, ed., *The Letters of Francis Thompson* (New York: Hawthorn Books, 1969) 29-30.

19 George Santayana, *The Middle Span* (London: Constable, 1947) 66.

20 Richard Le Gallienne, *The Romantic '90s* (New York: Doubleday, Page and Co., 1926) 188, 191.

21 Lionel Johnson, "Incurable," *The Pageant*, I, n.p. 1896, 131-133.

22 Lionel Johnson, *Some Letters to Richard Le Gallienne* (Edinburgh: Tregara Press, 1979) 8.

23 Walter Pater, *Marius the Epicurean: His Sensations and Ideas*, vol. I (London: Macmillan and Co., 1910) 49.

24 Walter Pater, "Wordsworth," *Appreciations* (New York: Macmillan, 1910) 62; *The Renaissance* (London: Macmillan, 1910) 236.

25 R. K. R. Thornton, *The Decadent Dilemma* (London: Edward Arnold Ltd., 1983) 116-117.

26 Schopenhauer, *Pensees, Maximas et Fragments*, transl. Burdeau (Paris: Bailliere, 1880) 74.

27 Frantz Fanon, *The Wretched of the Earth* (New York: Grove Press, 1968) 41. See also *Black Skin, White Masks* New York: Grove Press, 1967).

28 Abdul JanMahomed, *Manichean Aesthetics: The Politics of Literature in Colonial Africa* (Amherst: The University of Massachusetts Press, 1983) 3-4.

29 Scott Hughes Myerly, "The Eye Must Entrap the Mind: Army Spectacle and Paradigm in Nineteenth-Century Britain,"*Journal of Social History* 26.1 (Fall 1992): 105-107.

30 Viola Meynell, *Francis Thompson and Wilfrid Meynell: A Memoir* (London: Hollis and Carter, 1952) 40.

31 Francis Russell, *My Life and Adventure* (London, n.p., 1923): 90-91.2

Chapter 5

The Clown's Grimace: Dylan Thomas and Response to Failure of Modern Man

In reading Modern poetry we are faced with the poet's attempts to grapple with words and her/his recognition of how words can fail. The Modern poem, in one sense, is the outcome of this experience of failure in the Western world. It grows out of a felt need to express something, a felt need to use words to express it in and, finally, a felt need to be put together by the reader. Each of these needs is fraught with blank spaces. Conscious of the very vulnerability of the creative effort, exposed to a highly analytical environment and to the constant failure of one analysis against another, the Modern Western poet balks at making easy equations. If obscurity is a characteristic of Modern poetry, it is also an expression of failure—that words fail, that meanings fail, that form fails, that even the poem itself fails. If Plato rejected poets from his Republic, Modern poets constantly undermine their own efforts. The Modern poem often seems to collapse into oblivion. The very concreteness and immediacy of the words and images used constantly highlight the Modern poet's distrust of abstract concepts. At the same time s/he is in constant confrontation with the disintegration of a concrete self-identity or a coherent world-view. S/He is like a circus performer who, aware of her/his own absurd risk-taking gestures, dares to expose her/himself to the ultimates.

An emerging persona in Modern poetry is that of the clown, often a figure of ridicule, even of self-ridicule. We can recognize the affinities of this clown figure with diverse European literary traditions—the buffoon of Aristophanes, the "Fool" of Shakespeare, the bumbling hero of the Picaresque tradition, the self-parodying narrator of Lawrence Sterne, the highly dramatic, introspective Browning persona, and so on. But an important aspect of the Modern persona is her/his collapsing of the profound and the bathetic, of an intense individuality and ultimately, the projection of several masked selves; in Britain it grows out of the Modern poet's attraction to and withdrawal from the religio-poetic fervor in the latter part of the nineteenth century—a period in which poets like Hopkins, Thompson, and Johnson confronted the conflicts and paradoxes of the human body and the divine soul, the material and spiritual concerns which shape and break the self. In the early twentieth century, a revived interest in Donne and the Metaphysicals developed, mainly due to the practicing credo of the New Critics who valued poems with dramatic conflicts and complex images. The interest in Hopkins' poetry was often, therefore, linked to the emerging interest in complexity and obscurity which demanded searching analysis of images and constraining oppositions in the structure of the poems. Yet Hopkins' impact on Modern poetry goes deeper; we can realize the connections when we place Hopkins not as an isolated figure, but as one who headed the late-nineteenth-century literary attempts at expressing and addressing the religio-socio-political dilemma of Western man caught in his "mean house, bone house" yet aspiring for the heavens. Therefore, the study of Hopkins alongwith his contemporaries, with particular emphasis on their personae, brings a renewed understanding of the historical evolution of British literary Modernism. The Moderns, for the most part, rejected theology with an ironical gesture yet yearned for a ritual of some kind, rebuffed a given God but could not live without imaging the self as a kind of God, undermined the hortatory efforts of British imperialism to create success out of failure by irony, parody and clowning; yet in the very figure of the absurd hero, Modern Western man (often excluding the woman) confronted the meaning of his existential destiny within the parameters of a West-centered universe.

Modernism, in the context of the present study, needs to be examined as a period term for a cultural epoch, an aesthetic phenomenon, and an ideological project. Postmodernism, with its own ideological and epistemological underpinnings, has provided a substantive critique of Modernism, exposing the philosophic and political nature of its stance.

Post-structuralists, ranging from Charles Olson, Alain Robbe-Grillet, Susan Sontag, Ihab Hassan, John Barth, to Leslie Fiedler, including Francois Lyotard, Richard Rorty, Ernesto Laclau and Chantal Mouffe, have critiqued the aesthetic and ideological practices of Modernism.[1] These practices have often taken the form of political ambivalence and complicity with the Western male cultural dominants and discourses of autonomous subjectivity and universality. As Patricia Waugh in *Practising Postmodernism/Reading Modernism* sums up:

> "Postmodernism" now expresses the sense of a new cultural epoch in which distinctions between critical and functional knowledge break down as capitalism, in its latest consumerist phase, invades everything including the aesthetic, the post-colonial world and the unconscious (what Lionel Trilling had seen as that bit of biology radically opposed to culture), leaving no remaining oppositional space.[2]

Neil Larsen in *Modernism and Hegemony: A Materialist Critique of Aesthetic Agencies* exposes the underlying political narratives, what he calls "displaced politics," of modernist aesthetic theory and practice, in the wake of Fredric Jameson's significant work, *The Political Unconscious: Narrative as a Socially Symbolic Act*.[3] He views modernism as an ideological project, comprising "not only the literary-artistic canon but a wide array of theoretical discourses from aesthetics to philosophy, culture, and politics" (xxii). In his materialist critique, Larsen focuses on the links between modernism and a "crisis of representation" that affected all aspects of life in the late nineteenth century:

> This crisis, I further speculate, is the result of the modernization of capital itself during the nineteenth century, especially in the period leading up to the transformation of "classical" free market capitalism into monopoly/state capitalism and imperialism....Thus the "crisis in representation" also entails a "crisis in agency": the sense that social and historical agency is exercised by subjects linked to society as a whole by representational bonds of identity—what we might characterize, using the contemporary jargon, as an epical "master narrative" or "grand narrative" of History—falters in the face of events that indicate that the traditional "heroes" have been usurped by anonymous forces. Modernism stems from this crisis—which in

turn grasps as stemming from an intrinsic falsity residing in a purely conceptual operation, representation—and inverts it. (xxiv)

Larsen traces the growth of Modernism to the breakup of social and historical agency and the "resultant loosening of ties between individuals and society," and further demonstrates the rationale behind Modernism's claim upon the aesthetic, and its ascription of historical agency to "works of art":

> But modernism is not ready to relinquish the epical master narrative that is now threatened with dissolution. Agency must be retained, despite the apparent evacuation of the political. It is at this point, then, that modernism lays hand to the *aesthetic* and specifically to the (modern) "work of art," which alone among the postpolitical or subpolitical practices appears to hold out the promise of an oppositional synthesis. (xxiv)

Among the Modern poets, Dylan Thomas, like W. B. Yeats, exemplifies the tensions that reflect and in many ways problematize the Modernist ideological project. His poetry is grounded on the polarities of life/death, creation/destruction, particular/universal, reality/dream, conscious/unconscious, fertility/sterility—polarities that New Critics focused on. However, Thomas' poems also work out complex issues of identity within an underlying nationalist impulse and Welsh landscape, complicated often by his sympathies for the "English" cause in the critical war times. Thomas hoped to draw the "crudities, doubts, and confusions" of his day through a crucible of the Welsh faith in rituals, myths and magic as Yeats did with Irish mythology. In the "Note" to *The Collected Poems* Thomas observes:

> I read somewhere of a shepherd who, when asked why he made, from within fairy rings, ritual observances to the moon to protect his flocks, replied: "I'd be a damn' fool if I didn't!" These poems, with all their crudities, doubts, and confusions, are written for the love of Man and in praise of God, and I'd be a damn' fool if they weren't.[4]

Any discussion of Dylan Thomas as a Modern poet needs to be framed within the context of the Anglo-American literary movement of Modernism as well as the cultural complex of Anglo-Welsh writing. I will briefly examine some of the influential figures of this period, highlighting the shared as well as differing qualities of the writers, as they are significant to the analysis of Dylan Thomas' poetry.

W. B. Yeats, Ezra Pound and T. S. Eliot are three major Modern figures who created a kind of poetry in which the male persona and his various masks are the crucial experiencing centers. In Hopkins, Thompson, and Johnson we traced the dimension of human and divine conflicts within the evolving figure of the persona. One noticeable feature of the late-nineteenth-century poet's preoccupation was to explore the persona's split nature, his psychological tensions and conscious self-examination; however, despite the agitation of his mind and soul, the persona was a definable entity. A significant affirmation of self's success through failure was maintained by drawing the reader's attention to the self's yearning for such affirmation. In their creation of the poetic male persona, the duality and complexity of his nature were developed as necessary aspects of the persona's evolution to an identifiable human condition. Yeats, on the other hand, set out to formulate his doctrine of the self and the anti-self, which impacted a recognition of cultural as well as gender differences but often in terms of oppositions that paradoxically simplified and problemetized universalizing tendencies in Modernist discourse. These formulations, especially delineated as "Mask" and "Anti-Mask" images, engendered an approach which was to influence the Modern male poet's distancing of his motivations, personalities and complexities from those of the persona. Thus the poetic persona as the "Mask" or "the second self" was given an existence independent from the poet's.[5]

Another characteristic of the Modern poetic persona as worked out in the poetry of Yeats, Pound, and Eliot is its tragicomic nature. Unlike Hopkins' persona whose intense experience of the human will and divine aspiration overcomes the moments of self-ridicule, the Modern poetic persona dwells on his own absurdity and plays up his existential dilemma by assuming the mask of a clown figure, similar to but also different from the decadent poseur. Whereas the decadent persona celebrates his pose of failure, he is doing so as a kind of challenge. He accepts failure, but as an act, not as a reality. The modern clown-persona partly accepts the limitations of life as a reality, but his acceptance is marked by a vision of life as a dark comedy. Walter Kerr in *Tragedy and Comedy* exposes the existential dilemma of the clown in modern times:

> For us the tragic landscape has become virtually invisible....The clown, staring at it for inspiration and knowing that he must take all of his own sustenance from what he sees outside himself, can only have had the sensation of going slowly blind. The landscape has darkened. What can comedy do but grow darker with it?...But what drives comedy to desperation in our own time is something deeper than darkness. The tragic landscape is now described as a place that never truly existed, or at least a place that is not going to exist in future. Thus it claps down into utter blackness. On the instant comedy turns black with it.[6]

In Yeats, a striking persona who acts out the human failure—loss of youth's beauty and idealism—is the stuttering, bumbling caricature of old age. The comical, senile persona in Yeats' later poetry is a condensation of the imaginary figures he had created and of the figures from Irish mythology—Fergus, king of the Red Branch, seeking to "learn the dreaming wisdom" of the Druid but caught within the "great webs of sorrow" and left with the cry "But now I have grown nothing, knowing all"[7]; Aengus, the beautiful young man who has become "old with wandering/Through hollow lands and hilly lands" in search of beauty and love (*CPY*, 57); Oisin who is punished, for desiring the human world, with old age and its accompanying indignities: "A creeping old man...with the spittle on his beard" (*CPY* 379). An early Yeatsian image in the comic mode is Cuchulain who appears both in Yeats' poetry and cycle of plays (*on Baile's Strand, The Green Helmet, At the Hawk's Well, The Only Jealousy of Emer,* and *The Death of Cuchulain*). In "The Silver Laughter of Wisdom: Joyce, Yeats, and Farce," Cynthia D. Wheatley-Lovoy explores Joyce and Yeats' fascination with the comic and its vital relationship to the nature of modern heroism."[8] Joyce and Yeats viewed "comedy as a powerful weapon against social atrophy" (21), a weapon by which "to demonstrate the instability of their societies.... in which institutions and social positioning are being defined and redefined as well" (27), to parody the "xenophobia," the irish "mistrust of strangers" and "narrow conventions of truth" (28-29), to represent the "commodification of heroism" in "traditional heroic discourses" (32). Wheatley-Lovoy argues that "Bloom and Cuchulain qualify as comic heroes because they show their weaknesses as well as their strength to withstand life's contigencies" (34). In later poetry, Yeats affrims the "joyous energy," the "theatrical element" of the mask (*Mythologies* 334). This joyous energy, however, ennervates both the passion and intensity of reconciling "failed revolt" and "terrible beauty." Cuchulain "suffers defeat through which he gains sóme supernatural vision" (Wheatley-Lovoy 24).

In "Sailing to Byzantium," the aged persona's self-description is marked by both bathos and pathos: "An aged man is but a paltry thing,/A tattered coat upon a stick" (*CPY* 191). In "The Tower," the persona's description of self as a "caricature" is part of a painful self-questioning and self-pity. The absurd figure with old age tied to his back is debased to the non-human level ("As to a dog's tail"), a kind of Swiftian bestial figure. Out of this self-image the persona articulates the horror of human life and the grotesque reality of his meaningless existence. This enactment of self-failure as a clown's performance occurs again and again in Yeats' poems. In "Among School Children," the persona is conscious of his own private versus public image. In "The Circus Animal's Desertion," the persona is "but a broken man" who once ran a circus show but now is left with self-recrimination and the desolation of old age, "the foul rag-and-bone shop of the heart" (*CPY* 336). However, in "Lapis Lazuli," as Wheatley-Lovoy points out, the "gay eyes of the Chinamen" represent "the power of gaiety to transcend the tragedies of history."[8] The mask reveals "Gaiety transforming all that dread" (*CPY* 292).

The clown's performance is built on the paradox of action and inaction. He mimics a bicyclist by pedalling his legs furiously, but he rides no bicycle, only the thin air. The absurdity lies in the constant play of action against inaction. Further, the clown is involved in a constant process of "doing" and "undoing"—he may climb a ladder but will eventually slip down and reach the original point as does Charles Chaplin in his films. This occupation, implicit in the clown-mask, provides illimitable outlets for the Modern poetic persona to express the absurdity of his own existence, while balancing the thin line between tragedy and comedy. The clown-mask implies another possibility for the poet—the clown is a performer, an artist who often uses mime and gesture; he is both a counterpart and a counterpoint to the poet who also is an artist but who uses words to express himself. Wheatley-Lovoy refers to this performative nature of the artist, "The artist, like the hero, is a performer whose masks change as often as the conditions of heroism dictate" (34). The image of the self, both as the artist and man, remains a central concern for Yeats. His is a new religion born out of mythical figures and "imaginary people."[9] In *Yeats: The Man and the Masks*, Richard Ellmann points out the emerging symbolism in Yeats' "Sailing to Byzantium" which is relevant to Yeats' preoccupation with personae:

> for an image is in the world of art as holy as a sage. God in the poem stands less in the position of the Christian God than in that of supreme artist, artificer of eternity and the holy fire; he is thus also the poet and the human imagination which is sometimes in Yeats' system described as the maker of all things.[10]

Yeats' major persona in his later poetry, the tragicomic figure of senility, replaces God, or rather, through his undying dreams and regrets becomes a different kind of god, a different kind of creative artist and maker—a clown who "thinks in a marrow-bone," who is "For the song's sake a fool," "A foolish, passionate man" (*CPY* 281) and ultimately, a figure who embraces humanity in all its follies, foibles, and earthly struggles.

Ezra Pound was another major poet whose constant preoccupation with personae or versions of the self became a way of defining the past in the light of the present, tradition in the light of contemporaneity. In his essay, "Vorticism," Pound elaborated his preoccupation with the "search for oneself" through creation of personae in his poems.[11]

Bertrans de Born, Sextus Propertius, Hugh Selwyn Mauberley, Ulysses are all personae, versions of the self, past figures who eventually become contemporaneous. K. K. Ruthven in *A Guide to Ezra Pound's 'Personae'* (1926) points out the significance of creating 'personae' for Pound: at one level, Pound associated the creation of personae with a "sort of metempsychosis"; further his personae from the past sound like his contemporaries, and this leads him to the conviction that since "all time is contemporaneous, the point of focus [is] the consciousness of the writer whose mind ranges backward and forward over many hundreds of years"; finally, "the creation of personae is a way of imposing order on the chaos of history and serves much in the same function as myth in *The Waste Land* or *Ulysses.*"[12]

Ezra Pound was obviously interested in creating personae who reflect at once their historic identity and their contemporaneous features. Thus, Propertius is the historical figure who resisted the pressure of the powerful Maecenas to write political and rhetorical poems and continued to write love poems. But he is also the young Pound-artist struggling to maintain his own artistic integrity. The cross-overs in time are reflected as shifts in the persona's language—from the archaic ("clear font," "Who hath taught") to the modern.[13]

The reader's awareness of the modernity of the persona is marked by tracing an ironic tone of self-mockery, a feature which recurs with greater force and persistence in "Hugh Selwyn Mauberley." The Propertius who prophesizes his end is a kind of "homeomorph" of the dual identity of the E. P. Mauberley persona.[14] Ruthven elaborates on this self-antiself mask in some detail:

> Self-analysis produced the two personae in the poem, Mauberley and E. P., each of whom is an oversimplification of radically different elements in Pound himself. E. P. is a sort of pragmatic person Pound would like to be, a man fully aware of his own historicity and working in difficult conditions at the task of restoring literature to a more central place than it holds at present in our civilization. Even in 1922, however, Pound feared...that he was basically a *tour d'ivoire* aesthete like Mauberley, a man inordinately and helplessly attached to "nacre and objets d'art" (*Letters*, p. 234), and therefore incapable of anything more urgent or strenuous than subjective reveries. (126)

Confronting the possible failure of one's artistic integrity in an age of cheap imitation, mechanical production, and commercialized civilization, the modern poet-persona's ultimate self-defense is irony, in which the self is the target, as much as the sordid modern world is (*SPEP* 63).

Besides, the persona emphasizes the prosaic triviality of the modern age by an ironic use of allusion. The hortatory exclamation to Apollo is followed by a quote from Pindar's *Olympian*. The grandeur of the line is undercut by the banal image of the "tin wreath": "What god, man, or hero/Shall I place a tin wreath upon!" (*SPEP* 63). The ironic force of the passage is summed up succinctly by Ruthven:

> In such instances, the quotation is inappropriate in a meaningful way: the confrontation of gods and tin wreaths, the contrast between the powerfully rhythmic and the flatly prosaic, persuade us that heroic action and heroic literature are equally anachronistic in our time. (4)

Exposed to the persona's wordplay, literary associations, classical allusions, ironic undercutting and parody, the reader reacts to him as if he was a modern "verbal clown" whose reality is constantly maintained by his historical identity.[15] Pound, in his own personae, developed an attribute of the modern fool whose romantic irony is as much a revelation of the self's failure as of the age; it was also an attribute which recurred in many of T. S. Eliot's poems.

Eliot's personae in the early poems and the tonal centers of "The Waste

Land" experience failure, often sexual failure, in the larger framework of social failure. J. Alfred Prufrock's "love song" is a desultory confession of ennui, vacuity and inaction: "Do I dare? Do I dare?"[16] Prufrock identifies himself as the anti-heroic figure, the "ridiculous" "Fool" or the intellectually agile Shakespearian Fool who spans all time (*CPE* 7). Tragic heroes have had their day; this is the age of the comic-pathetic "Fool." Underlining the self-mockery and parody is a strain of the prophetic, "the sage fool," the clown as truth-teller.[17] This strain marks the other tragi-farcical personae in Eliot's later poems.

The persona in "Gerontion" describes himself as an "old man" marked by inaction, sexual disease, loss of all senses and end of faith (*CPE* 21, 23). Yet, he, like Prufrock, is not wholly the insane clown; he can read the signs too, "the word within a word" (*CPE* 21). Sweeney, who appears and reappears in "Sweeney Erect," "Sweeney Agonistes" and "The Waste Land" is a sexually depraved figure. Struck by "the falling sickness," symbolic of the fallen state of man, Sweeney reflects the failure of Western civilization. His grotesque, absurd appearance confirms his affinity with the crude, base, buffoonish figure who has appeared as the literary "social parasite" since the second century in Greece and in Plutarch's accounts (Riggan 79). This lewd, obscene figure, however, is an evolving persona whose tragic nature the reader can perceive by linking him to Agamemnon, Orestes, and ironically, even Christ. In "Sweeney Among the Nightingales," Sweeney guards the "horned gate"—the gate of lechery, death, but also of truth. In "The Wasteland" Sweeney is not present as a persona but as a ghostly figure haunting the "Narcissus-exiled Israelite-Rousseauesque" persona of 'The Fire Sermon' section. Mrs. Porter and Sweeney appear in the unfinished poem "Sweeney Agonistes" as the "Queen of Hearts" and a possible "King of Clubs" respectively. In the "Fragment of an Agon" Sweeney also is a reminder that human life is nothing but birth, copulation and death (*CPE* 80, 84). The Sweeney-figure in 'The Fire Sermon' passage echoes both the depravity of the civilization as well as the prophecy of death in a series of mock-literary allusions to

Marvell's "To his Coy Mistress," *Day's Parliament of Bees*, and Verlaine's *Parsifal*, among others.

Eliot's own note on Tiresias and his central importance in "The Waste Land" is revealing:

> Tiresias, although a mere spectator and not indeed a "character" is yet the most important personage in the poem, uniting all the rest. Just as the one-eyed merchant, seller of currants, melts into the Phoenician Sailor, and the latter is not wholly distinct from Ferdinand Prince of Naples, so all the women are one woman, and the two sexes meet in Tiresias. What Tiresias *sees*, in fact, is the substance of the poem. (*CPE* 52)

As an experiencing center of the poem, Tiresias disrupts the briefly sketched, rapidly shifting gallery of personae, appearing often as fragmentary, disembodied voices. This feature is important in the structure of the whole poem, for Tiresias is an intrusion, an old misfit, a grotesque parody of sex (*CPE* 43-44).

It is the prophetic distance coupled with a human sympathy that makes Tiresias' voice a pervading consciousness, but Tiresias is not a wholly tragic figure. He is in many ways a comical misfit, and it is in this role that he humanizes the tawdry scene of modern sexuality and conveys echoes of neurotic fears, moral righteousness and cold cynicism: "one must be so careful these days," "what you get married for if you don't want children?" (*CPE* 39,42), culminating in the lines "She smoothes her hair with automatic hand,/ And puts a record on the gramophone" (*CPE* 44).

Eliot's peculiar use of "voices" in "The Waste Land" is not so much to create characters, but as Rosenthal and Gall point out in *The Modern Poetic Sequence*, "to build the poem's tonal centers."[18] It is, therefore, the volatile, rapid succession of voices, echoing and counterpointing each other, bawdy, ironic, poignant or indifferent that Tiresias' voice orchestrates. The reader in responding to the voices is involved in a kind of juggling act. His identification with each voice is brief, not sustained, yet the cumulative effect of the rapidly succeeding voices is to impress him with their own resonance. Thus, the reader, while believing that he can easily dissociate from each voice, is being pulled into a whirlpool from which he cannot escape so easily.

Yeats, Pound and Eliot each developed personae who are the key centers of their poems. They are both specific figures, in a certain age and civilization, shaped by individual experiences and historical forces, and also voices that collapse time and space in their own consciousness of the absurd comic-pathetic modern man creating his own reality in his own mind.

ii

Among the modern poets, a highly ingenious yet controversial figure who claimed the imagination and the fervent adulation (often filtered with intrigue, puzzlement and angry disappointment) of the Western readers and audiences in the thirties to the early fifties was Dylan Thomas. Much has been written about Dylan the bawdy, incongruous man, the sensational poet of birth, sex and death, and of course, the tongue-in-cheek bohemian philanderer out to shock the world and to rebel against his own Welsh non-conformist upbringing. What is of particular interest in the present context—the exploration of the Modern poets' responses to the experience of failure—is Dylan Thomas' use of different roles and innumerable masks in order to project a highly riddling persona in an equally riddling world of paradoxes.

A passage from Thomas' letter to Pamela Hansford Johnson, dated 25 December 1933, may be taken as one explanation for his incessant preoccupation with different personae in his poetry:

> Think how much wiser we would be if it were possible for us to change our angles of perspective as regularly as we change our vests: a certain period would be spent in propelling ourselves along our backs, in order to see the sky properly and all the time; and another period in drifting belly-downwards through the air in order to see the earth. As it is, this perpetual right-angle of ours leads to a prejudiced vision.[19]

David Holbrook, the psychoanalytic biographer-critic of Dylan Thomas, employs object-relations psychoanalysis in *Dylan Thomas: The Code of Night* and concludes that Thomas' role-playing stems from the schizoid persona's fear of loss of identity.[20] The extensive exploration of Freudian psychoanalysis to accommodate one's cultural experiences leads Holbrook to some very acute observations about Thomas' obviously problematic personality. But it is unsatisfactory, or at least incomplete, in that it does not account for Thomas' artistic dexterity in creating various masks and his conscious manipulation of the poetic personae in a search not only for his personal identity but for human identity as well.

Thomas' own words about his desire to escape a "prejudiced vision" and the wisdom of changing "our angles of perspective" are supported by his constant efforts to escape the narrow moral code of his Welsh upbringing. He constantly plays on sexual innuendoes, puns, often blatant ribaldry and puckish candor in the persona of the bohemian rebel. FitzGibbon, in *The Life of Dylan Thomas*, touches on the resources of this persona as a combination of both sympathy and cunning: "This ability to present his very strong personality in so many different guises contains within itself both the most marvelous and enriching sympathy as well as a low and despicable cunning—and all the gradations that lie between."[21] The curious but highly characteristic tension between genuine sympathy and diabolic cunning pervades all of Thomas' personae, coming to an explosive reconciliation in the figure of the clown. Georg M. A. Gaston, in *Dylan Thomas: A Reference Guide*, comments on Paul Ferris' 1977 biography as a work that "attempts to separate the facts from the legends surrounding the poet's life"; its research "suggests that the poet manufactured a 'character for the world to be entertained by, part-poet and part-clown,' that the 'two went together' and that the 'borderline between fact and fiction may have been blurred'."[22] I will explore this figure of the clown as the central persona in Thomas' poetry.

The chief characteristic of the bohemian-rebel persona is a reckless, adventurous spirit. No doubt Thomas had seen himself as a "provincial bohemian," leaving Wales for London as a gesture of revolt: "The land of my fathers. My fathers can keep it."[23] In his unfinished story, "The Adventures in the Skin Trade," the rebel-hero, Samuel Bennet escapes from the prosaic, secure life of his parents: "In the biggest bedroom overlooking the field that was called the back, his father turned over the bills of the month in his one dream; his mother in bed mopped and polished through a wood of kitchens. He closed the door: now there was nobody to disturb him."[24] But his leave-taking is not so simple or innocent; it is destructive in its rebellious tearing up of his mother's snapshot, smudging his father's history sheets with a charcoal, and breaking the china set (*CS* 241). The whole point of the destructive acts is to confirm his own self-banishment as final, irrevocable: "Come and look at Samuel Bennet destroying his parents' house in Mortimer Street, off Stanley's Grove; he will never be allowed to come back" (*CS* 242). It is an expression of what John Logan, in "Dylan Thomas and the Ark of Art," refers to as "the floods of destruction he found in himself" and from which his art provided a safe refuge, "his art as an ark," "his temporary peace."[25] The bleary-eyed adolescent Samuel Bennet's sexual fantasying is another deliberate mark of rebellion against the structures of the Swansea moral code.

The bohemian-rebel personae that occur in Thomas' poems project different aspects of the Samuel Bennet figure—anger, cynicism, rashness, vitality, exuberance, pugnacity, self-confidence, but also guilt and shame. A recurring quality of these personae is a constant obsession with sex as both a life-giving and a life-denying feature of the human identity. The young boys of "I See the Boys of Summer" are the rebel figures, "the dark deniers" who challenge the seasons, who can destroy creation and create from destruction.[26] Celebrating life and death in the phallic symbol of the "poles of promise," the bohemian-rebel figures abandon themselves to nature. Echoing the jaunty "hey, ho" from the song of the clown in Shakespeare's *The Twelfth Night*, the boys celebrate their own image of self as a kind of wise fool[27]: "In spring we cross our foreheads with the holly,/Heigh ho the blood and berry" (*CP* 3). One of the pervading self-images of the bohemian-rebel persona is that of the "tough guy," projected either as the "sons of flint and pitch" (*CP* 3) or as the highly tense physical dynamo with the "jawbone riven" and "the flesh's lock and vice" revolting against the mechanical "jointed lever" and "screws" (*CP* 39), a kind of the Hopkinsian Harry Ploughman figure whose stance is to defy the power of poetic, social, political or sexual conformity (*CP* 38).

Another recurring image of the free-spirited persona is that of the self as dog. In the collection of stories titled *Portrait of the Artist as a Young Dog*, the young boy is a vital, spirited being with a strong affinity for the world of senses:

> I felt all my young body like an excited animal surrounding me, the torn knees bent, the bumping heart, the long heat and depth between the legs, the sweat prickling in the hands, the little balls of dirt between the toes, the eyes in the sockets, the tucked-up voice, the blood racing, flying, jumping, swimming, and waiting to pounce. There, playing Indians in the evening, I was aware of me myself in the exact middle of a living story, and my blood was my adventure and my name. I sprang with excitement and scrambled up through the scratching brambles again. (*CS* 132)

Performing his "sensual strut," the dog-man persona perceives the outer and the inner regions through keen sensitivity to sensations, as evident in "Before I Knocked" and the notebook versions of "How Shall My Animal."[28] Other poems, such as "A Process in the Weather" and "As Yet Ungotten," emphasize the personae's world of sensory responses (*CP* 7, 8). In "My Hero Bares his Nerves," the mock-heroic figure deliberately plays on the multi-leveled imagery of the poet's ego, hand or phallus: "My hero bares his nerves along my wrist/That rules from wrist to shoulder" (11). Commenting on the last line, "He pulls the chain, the cistern moves," William York Tindall in *A Reader's Guide to Dylan Thomas* sums it up as implying that "masturbation, writing a poem, and defecation are parallel and of equal value....This poem cleans up darkness by bringing it to the light of ribald comedy."[29] This constant upsetting of the serious, often philosophical subject-matter (such as birth, procreation, death, human identity and loss of it, passage of time, and human suffering) by a kind of bawdy, puckish humor is characteristic of the bohemian-artist of animal spirits. The "young dog" image in the *Portrait* stories and its variations in Thomas' personae, the "boily boy," the wind chaser, and the spirited poet of the physical senses suggest certain characteristics. Richard A. Davies in his article, "Dylan Thomas' Image of the 'Young Dog' in the *Portrait*" points out some of these traits:

> The stance Dylan Thomas chose to emphasize in his *Portrait* stories, that of a "young dog," evokes an image of bravado, defiance and aggression in the face of life, a devil-may-care approach to existence that would seem to be well suited to Thomas' fertile comic fancy. I use the word "seem" because a reader would be insensitive to Thomas' version of life if he failed to see the irony of the "young dog" pose. There is a pattern in Thomas' parade of youthful versions of himself.... one of a gradual loss of courage and boldness, a consequent increase in fears and terrors, until the young dog is fully metamorphosed into a "terrified prig of a love-mad young man...."[30]

The outer mask of bravado which hides the fears and sexual innocence of the adolescent in the *Portrait* stories, like "The Fight," "Extraordinary Little Cough," "Just Like Little Dogs," is a projection of Thomas' own identification with the dog-figure in life. In one of his letters to Vernon Watkins, dated 15 July 1937, Thomas dwells on self-recrimination by a sustained image of self as a cringing dog.[31] The extremes of self-aplomb and self-denigration in the personae, as in Thomas' life, are humanized by comic exaggeration. If much of Thomas' poetry has been criticized as adolescent and immature, the fact remains that he *is* concerned with the limitations of human beings at their most critical period, adolescence, a period when the self is emerging from the conflicts of 'id' and 'ego.' Freud had exposed the horrifying implications of childhood maladjustments in his psychoanalytic theories; Dylan Thomas wished to go further. Through comic parody and a kind of Swiftian, incisive juxtaposition of the human ego and his animal nature, Thomas cut both ends—he made the Freudian theories realistic, human and even, at times, laughable because they were so much a part of human nature; at the same time, the ironic self-display counterpoints the easy, humorous acceptance of self with a recurrent, clinical appraisal in the moments of self-failure. Regarding this concern, Kenneth Seib, in "*Portrait of the Artist as a Young Dog*: Dylan's *Dubliners*," links Dylan to Joyce, "an author from whom Thomas borrowed heavily."[32] Besides noting the autobiographical content, the achronological time sequence, the overall unity, use of local color, and similarity in titles (referring to Joyce's *Portrait of the Artist as a Young Man*), Seib argues:

> Finally, Thomas' stories employ much of the same symbolism found in Joyce's *Portrait*: sea, circle, light, dark, sermon, and dog. One even suspects "dog" of being a Joycean anagram for "God"; thus Thomas' title implies that his fictional Dylan is, all told, a young god become one more Welsh whelp fallen into dog days. His *Portrait*, like much of his poetry, recapitulates the Fall. (141)

In the episode, "Extraordinary Little Cough," the "young dog" persona painfully tries to be like Brazell and Skully, the "two big bullies," and thus escapes from the reticence and sexual fears of the "poor little Cough," a part of his own self. The embarrassing moment when his cap drops, while he is being introduced to three young girls, is reflective of adolescent experiences of inadequacy (*CS* 171).

Thomas' first published poem, "The Song of the Mischievous Dog" is in the derivative mode of his Grammar School magazine publishing days. Yet it is significant that he begins this piece of humorous verse with the line, "There are many who say that a dog has its day."[33] Among his early drafts (most of them remain unpublished as poems) from his *Notebooks* is the poem "Sweet as [a dog's] kiss night sealed," in which the dog image is associated with tenderness, peace and kindness (Maud, ed. 163). Opposed to the dog image and its life-preserving qualities are the destructive animal images of maggots, vultures, vampires and ghosts. The personae in Thomas' poetry do not always associate youthful innocence with the dog image. As seen in the projections of the adolescent's inner feelings, conflicts and sexual confusions, there is a dark comedic streak in the personae's identification with or dissociation from their animal nature. In "Out of the Sighs" the persona regrets that man has nothing to give; his sterility, his inability to offer, if not love, anything at all, is man's "perpetual defeat." In this context, he evokes the dog-man image: "Groping for matter under the dog's plate,/Man should be cured of distemper" (*CP* 57). In other poems, such as "My World is Pyramid," the shapeless, unborn persona, the Shandian figure, often describes the process of his conception and creation in images of the bestiary, devoid of the free-spirited dog image (39). In "Before I Knocked and Flesh Let Enter," the images of the worm and the maggot link the unborn foetus persona to the cycle of death-in-life: "My heart knew love, my belly hunger;/I smelt the maggot in my stool" (9). The human self, at times a dog figure, at times a worm, ranges among all evolutionary scales in order to comprehend its own identity and destiny. Perhaps the most striking image of the evolving persona occurs in the first sonnet of the sequence, "Altarwise by Owl-Light": "...a dog among the fairies,/...Bit out the mandrake with to-morrow's scream" (80). Tindall concludes that the movement in this section is towards the birth of "Thomas, the young creative devil-dog mandrake," for Thomas was a reporter for the Swansea paper at one time and could be said to have had "a jaw for news" (Tindall 129). The mandrake legend is explicated by H. H. Kleinman in *The Religious Sonnets of Dylan Thomas*:

> The mandrake has a bifurcated root, giving the appearance of a tiny human form. It was rare, valuable, and dangerous to obtain. Medieval legend endowed it with the power to induce fecundity and assuage pain. In order to uproot a mandrake one had to avoid being within hearing distance of its fatal scream; therefore, a dog was tied to a mandrake root and lured forward to grab the food, pulling the mandrake out of the earth; and at that moment the piercing deadly scream of the mandrake killed the dog.[34]

The reader is confronted with images that move from the Biblical sphere to the present world of journalism and back to legend and myth. Further, the reader must unravel the words "altarwise" and "owl light" to see that they are compounds or words, parts of which have been transposed—"altarlight" and "owlwise." Engaged in an activity of perpetual cross-transference, the reader is prepared for the dog-poet persona's own movement from the stance of the observer and reporter to that of an active participant. In proclaiming the story of the Nativity, the dog-poet must go through a kind of death for the birth of Christ or his own heart. The persona as "a dog among the fairies" echoes Eliot's phrase, "Sweeney Among the Nightingales." Sweeney, in Eliot's poem, is a figure of sordid animality whose coarseness is a contrast to the mythic reminders of spiritual beauty, the "nightingales" singing in the background (*CPE* 35-36). By associating himself with the "dog" image and with Sweeney, the Thomas persona blatantly claims to be no more than a figure of animal spirits. It is significant to recall that Sweeney, in Eliot's "Fragment of an Agon," had asserted that life is nothing but "Birth, and copulation, and death"; so does the dog-poet persona in Thomas' poem.

Furthermore, Kleinman's identification of dog with Christ, "the hound of Heaven, who bites out the mandrake (man) from the fork or loins of Abaddon, thus redeeming man from sin (Adam) and death (Abaddon)" is justifiable (19). The poetic persona in Thomas' poem "Foster the Light" addresses God to "pluck a mandrake music from the marrowroot" (*CP* 69). Moreover, the image of God as the "hound of Heaven" must have impressed him for he often acknowledged the influence of Francis Thompson; the image of the mandrake might have been influenced by Donne's use of it in "Go and Catch a Falling Star," or "The Progress of the Soule." The image is also recurrent in Shakespeare's plays (*Romeo and Juliet*, IV.iii.37; *Anthony and Cleopatra*, I.v.4; *Henry IV*, part II, I.ii.17; III.ii.339; VI.ii.310) (Kleinman 132).

Dylan Thomas must have been aware of the intriguing fact that "dog" spelt backwards would read "god," as his playfulness with words makes clear. David Clay Jenkins points out in his article:

> He had a love of words. He liked to twist them delightfully around, roll them and bowl them...He was delighted at subtitling himself for an advertising man: The Ugly Suckling; and astonished when he once found on a menu that 'live' backward spelt 'evil.' It must have been this playfulness with words that caused the boily boy to toy with his own name on the back of one of the notebooks: "Samoth Nalyd" (his name spelt backwards).[35]

The identification of poetic persona with dog and god (as Christ), justifiable on grounds of sacrificial deaths that each undergoes, is also achieved by explosive verbal clowning.

To understand the significance of the roles played by the poetic personae, in Thomas' poetry, it is essential to keep in mind that its intrinsic quality is one of clowning. It is a quality that the Modern poetic persona has come to adopt in the face of an age with few sustaining traditions—an age of comic-pathetic gestures rather than of any overwhelming tragic acts. Thomas' clown persona is an "Enfant Terrible" figure, a combination of the wildly "wicked" bohemian-rebel and the innocent, childlike druid-bard, a prophet and a pacifist—a figure who holds in himself the composite of contrarieties, even as Thomas felt he did: "I hold a beast, an angel and a madman in me" (FitzGibbon, ed., *Selected Letters* 196). In the poem "My World is Pyramid," the persona is an unborn Shandian figure who relates the story of his own conception and birth with verbal and syntactical juggling; Tindall calls this juggling a kind of "metaphysical fun". "Plainer syntax could impair the gaiety, which, like the theme, requires a little darkness and something more than grotesque double rhymes: 'doubles...dabbles,' for instance, and 'bubbled...babbled'" (Tindall 71). The unborn persona describes himself as the "arterial angel" (*CP* 35), "the unborn devil" with an "angel's hood" (*CP* 37)—a product of the opposites described in "Incarnate Devil," "good" and "evil," God the "fiddling warden" of Eden and the "serpent" fiddling "in the shaping-time" (*CP* 46). The "fiddling" action of both God and the serpent recalls the infamous Nero fiddling while Rome was burning down. The persona's identification of himself as madman grows out of his parodic version of the creative-destructive forces working in Eden.

In his letter to Pamela Hansford Johnson, dated 9 May 1934, Thomas appraises himself as "a freak user of words, not a poet," "a fool like the hyena, sitting up till dawn without any pleasure, making a noise with his guts" (FitzGibbon, ed., *Selected Letters* 122-123). In another letter written to Marguerite Caetani, dated 6 November 1952, Thomas describes his own psychological response to fear as one of inflating his self-grandiose, "to bloat myself like a frog, to magnify my unimportance" (381).

The madman in Thomas' short story, "The Mouse and the Woman," has a brief vision of life as something wonderful through the "dark woman" of his dreams: "She pointed out bird and bush with her fingers, illuminating a new loveliness in the wings and leaves, in the sour churning of water over pebbles, and a new life along the dead branches of the trees" (*CS* 76). The linking of the subterranean levels of consciousness with the "dark woman," evoking Freudian analysis of female sexuality in terms of the "dark continent," implies both implicit and explicit conceptualization of gender and race differences in terms of boundaries that separate stages of human consciousness. These conceptualizations have, in turn, reinforced notions of the female or the racial other in terms of the exotic and/or the infantile. The madman, however, fails to keep his "miracle" and so "the miracle passed" (83). The madman is also a creative artist; as Modernists posited the terrain of the exotic "other" as a utopia for the recovery of the jaded mind and spirit of the Western man, the loss of his creation is through his own limitations: "He knew that he had failed before the eye of God and the eye of Sirius to hold his miracle" (85). The failure of the madman signals the distinction between the narrative of adventure and the narrative of the quest as it is inscribed in the modernist versions of colonialist discourses of exploration, discovery and appropriation of space. Chris Bongie analyzes the specific nature of this difference:

> What for the adventurer holds out the promise of a positive resolution takes on a very different meaning for the subject of the quest, to whom "the exotic and the

extraordinary are only ciphers for the essential aporia of every experience"....In the age of the New Imperialism, the exotic necessarily becomes for those who persist in search of it, the sign of an aporia—of a constitutional absence at the heart of what had been projected as a possible alternative to modernity. (22)

Although the writers of the fin de siècle gave voice to this sign, they also engaged in the "duplicitous act of simultaneously renouncing and, as it were, re-announcing the exotic, affirming and negating it" (22). In Modernist writers, "exoticism has been exhausted as an *ideology*, that is, as a discursive practice that still produces itself in the register of belief; yet, by means of the duplicitous strategy of allegory, they *rhetorically* conserve the exotic, engaging in a renewed, and strategic, dreaming of what they know to be no more (but no less) than a dream" (23).

A version of this madman appears in the poem, "Love in the Asylum." Here the madman persona lives in a house with "madhouse boards worn thin by [his] walking tears" (119). He too is visited by a girl "mad as birds." Here the persona, however, overcomes the failure that the madman in "The Mouse and the Woman" had experienced, and is enlightened to the mysteries of the world within the arms of his beloved (119).

The clown as the devil, the angel and the madman is a figure from convention. In the medieval plays the devil often appears as a clown; in Marlowe's *Faustus* the devil appears as a bumptious trickster. The angelic aspect of the clown is explicit in his universal hearty, good humored Santa Claus image—a lovable, childlike, innocent figure. The clown as madman is a kind of "the sottie clown" defined by William Riggan in *Picaros, Madmen, Naifs, and Clowns*:

> Yet inasmuch as...a sottie clown...annihilates reality, turns life into a game and the world upside down, and ends by creating chaos, there is something of a dark abyss beneath the whole elaborate joke; for the world inhabited by Harlequin and the sottie fool is irrational, menacing, and demonic. (97)

In Dylan Thomas' poems the devil-angel-madman clown persona is transformed into a modern man, fraught by nerves, limitations, failures and unique revelations, in search of his own identity. Whether expressing sexual abhorrence or indulgence, the bawdy, lewd court jester of the second-century Greek accounts underlies the complex persona exploring the creation and disintegration of the world and his own personality.

One of the crucial issues that the clown persona in Thomas' poems is responding to is his own failures—failure of the self to find reality, to find human value in others, and failure to feel. The connections among Thomas' stories, poems and the poetic play titled *Under Milk Wood* also lie in the persistence of certain images of this "failure." Kenneth Seib, regarding Thomas' stories, gives the example of "one Warm Saturday," which is "filled with images of death, drowning and destruction" and in which "Dylan's failure is complete" (144).

Outside Thomas' stories and poetry, some of the bumbling, clownish figures in his play, *Under Milk Wood*, find a human generosity towards their own feelings. Like Joyce's *Dubliners*, Thomas' play explores the lives of ordinary people living in the pastoral-magical setting of the Welsh countryside, called "Llaregyb." One of the characters, Eli Jenkins, voices the strain of normalcy in apparent madness and clownish foolery that Dylan Thomas had struggled to express throughout his career. Jenkins' portrayal exemplifies a fresh look at self and also a possibility to accept oneself for all one's human inadequacies and failures:

We are not wholly bad or good
Who live our lives under Milk Wood.[36]

In Thomas' poems, however, the various self-dramatizations of the persona are underlined by self-criticism. In "There was a Saviour," the persona begins with an observation about the strictures of religious beliefs which imprison the children. Then slowly, in the third stanza, he includes himself and the reader among the lost children, both victims and participants of a ritual that stultifies human feeling: "Now in the dark there is only yourself and myself" (*CP* 139). The tone of outrage is deflected, in the last line, towards "yourself" and "myself." The extreme opposite of this self-critical persona is the defiant rebel. Often the defiant persona is both comical and pathetic in his response to self-failure, as seen in the dog-man identity. The mixed attitude toward self is captured in the poem "Should Lanterns Shine." The motion and activity of the defiant self-critical persona as well as his poised waiting for the ball to come down constitute both heroic and mock-heroic gestures (*CP* 72).

The persona's failure to find human value in others is expressed as an inability to feel. In the story, "Adventures in the Skin Trade," this failure is expressed as a sexual impotence:

> on his first free days since he was born Samuel sat with a loose girl in a locked bathroom over a tea-shop, the dirty curtains were drawn, and his hand lay on her thighs. He did not feel any emotion at all. 0 God, he thought, make me feel something, make me feel as I ought to, here is something happening and I'm cool and dull as a man in a bus. (CS 269)

Before exploring the poetic personae's responses to failure in feeling, it is interesting to trace the autobiographical truth underlying Thomas' presentation of Samuel's character and then see how he reworks a different kind of poetic persona. A letter Thomas wrote to Trevor Hughes at the time of his aunt Ann Jones' death reveals his consciousness of his own failure to feel:

> But the foul thing is I feel utterly unmoved, apart....There must be something lacking in me. I don't feel worried, or hardly ever, about other people. It's self, self, all the time....Is this, he pondered, a lack of soul? (FitzGibbon, ed. *Selected Letters* 11-12)

A kind of "clown-against-the-universe," the Samuel-Dylan complex is "an outsider, an artful dodger," and in many ways one aspect of the Charles Chaplin figure—the agile, circuitous caricature who wishes to avoid "what he knows will defy him" (Kerr 197-199). Thomas often acknowledged that

Charles Chaplin was one of his heroes.[37] The other aspect of the Chaplin figure—the wise tramp with an abundance of feeling—is what gains development in the following poetic personae. Often this sympathetic aspect grows out of the earlier mask of the "sly opportunist" or the two masks appear as the opposing natures of two dramatic personae.

The attitudes of cynicism and denial of feeling and the human alternatives to such attitudes are explored in the poem "Find Meat on Bones." Here the father's advice to the son is one of "carpe diem," enjoy youth while it lasts (*CP* 74). But the son, through the experience of pain and heartbreak in following his father's advice, questions the life of careless sensations:

> I cannot murder, like a fool,
> Season and sunshine, grace and girl,
> Nor can I smother the sweet waking."
> (*CP* 75)

The persona in "Out of the sighs" goes beyond rebellion. His response is one of giving:

> For all there is to give I offer:
> Crumbs, barn, and halter.
> (*CP* 57)

His act of giving, however feeble or comically surreptitious, is one way of redeeming "some certainty" out of his "perpetual defeat" (*CP* 56). In "The Conversation of Prayer," the mature man's awareness of the powers of love and death and the child's indifference to them are contrasted. The man on the stairs, "full of tears" for the dying woman whom he loves, is rewarded with the warmth of her presence. On the other hand, the child going to bed, "not caring to whom he climbs his prayer," finds his own nemesis: He "shall drown in a grief as deep as his made grave" even as he is dragged "to one who lies dead" (111).

In the poem "Lament," the "windy boy" persona recalls his own outrageous "wickedness" with dark humor; he sees himself as a heartless youth who wooed and left many girls. However, the persona grows out of this image of the self as callous, "To find a woman's soul for a wife" (*CP* 195).

The finest, most sustaining persona who lives out his true feelings is the boy mourning his aunt's death in "After the Funeral." Comparing this poem to the previously quoted letter of Thomas to Trevor Hughes at the time of his aunt's death, the reader notices a complete reversal of character portrayal—the unfeeling boy of the letter is transformed into the only sincere mourner among other hypocrites with their "mule praises, brays,/Windshake of sailshaped ears" (96). The persona, "Ann's bard on a raised earth" offers his own self-consciously inadequate but sincere memorial to his aunt. In a wealth of images recalling the natural landscape of Wales, he pays tribute to Ann, an intrinsic inhabitant of the "worlds of Wales": "Bless her bent spirit with four, crossing birds" (96).

The transformation of the "fool" to the "wise" self implies the process of self-making. The "wise fool" image is a significant mask because it is so different from the Dylan-Samuel identity. Usually, the Dylan-Samuel poetic personae have much in common and are often reflections of each other. But here the departure is an evidence of Thomas' ability to create personae who reflect the unexplored depths of feeling that he possessed but often feared to expose. This evidence also modifies Holbrook's assertion that Thomas' "poems are part of the disguise against the contact that would destroy," that is, the contact with the reality of his own inner self (205).

The "wise fool" image of the poetic persona projects a positive response to self-failure. However, it is not the final gesture or even the only gesture in Thomas' poetry. There is always the devilish, wicked practical joker who cannot help but ridicule any signs of transformation in himself, "And all the deadly virtues plague my death!" (*CP* 196).

Dylan Thomas' poetry is rich in the variety of personae who act out the comic-pathetic condition of modern man—a condition which the American poet E. E. Cummings explored in his poems and plays through the verbal acrobats and wily playfulness of the spunky little "i." In Cummings' play "Him," the character called Him compares an artist to a circus performer astride three chairs placed one on top of each other and balanced on a high wire. The three chairs proclaim the identity of the clown-acrobat figure: "I am an Artist, I am a Man, I am a Failure."[38] So do the personae in Dylan Thomas' poetry declare the duality, and often the multiplicity, of their identity:

> I, in my intricate image, stride on two levels
> Forged in man's minerals...
> My half ghost in armour hold hard in death's
>   corridor,
> To my man-iron sidle. (*CP* 40)

Notes

1 Francois Lyotard, *The Postmodern Condition* (Minneapolis: University of Minnesota Press, 1984; Richard Rorty, *Consequences of Pragmatism: Essays 1972-1980* (Minneapolis: University of Minnesota Press, 1982); Ernesto Laclau and Chantal Mouffe, *Hegemony and Socialist Strategy: Towards a Radical Democratic Politics* (London: Verso, 1985).

2 Patricia Waugh, *Practising Postmodernism/Reading Modernism* (New York: Edward Arnold, 1992), 5.

3 Neil Larsen, *Modernism and Hegemony: A Materialist Critique of Aesthetic Agencies* (Minneapolis: University of Minnesota Press, 1990), xxii. Fredric Jameson in *The Political Unconscious: Narrative as a Socially Symbolic Act* (Ithaca: Cornell University Press, 1981) provides an Althusserian analysis of the Marxist concept of production, whereby he views literary works as "symbolic acts," the products of "various coexisting modes of productions" and ideological conflict (87, 97).

4 Dylan Thomas, *The Collected Poems of Dylan Thomas, 1934-1952* (New York: New Directions Books, 1957), xiii.

5 W. B. Yeats, *Mythologies* (New York: Macmillan, 1959) 334.

6 Walter Kerr, *Tragedy and Comedy* (New York: Simon and Schuster, 1967) 317.

7 W. B. Yeats, *The Collected Poems* (New York: Macmillan, 1956) 379.
Note: Further quotes from the above text will be indicated by the contraction *CPY* followed by page numbers in parenthesis.

8 Cynthia D. Wheatley-Lovoy, "'The Silver Laughter of Wisdom': Joyce, Yeats, and Heroic Farce," *South Atlantic Review* 58.4 (Nov. 1993): 20.

9 W. B. Yeats, *Autobiographies* (London: Macmillan, 1955) 116.

10 Richard Ellmann, *Yeats: The Man and the Masks* (New York: E. P. Dutton, 1948) 254.

11 Ezra Pound, "Vorticism," *Fortnightly Review* XCVI:573 (Sept. 1914): 464.

12 K. K. Ruthven, *A Guide to Ezra Pound's 'Personae'* (Berkeley: University of California Press, 1969) 8-9.

13 Ezra Pound, *Selected Poems* (New York: New Directions, 1957) 78.
    Note: Further quotes from the above text will be indicated by the contraction *SPEP* followed by page numbers in parenthesis.

14 Hugh Kenner, *The Pound Era* (Berkeley: University of California Press, 1971) 33.

15 William Riggan, *Picaros, Madmen, Naifs, and Clowns: The Unreliable First-Person Narrator* (Norman: University of Oklahoma Press, 1981) 102. Riggan deals mainly with novels, but his identification of the different kinds of clown figures and his terminology can be applied to several personae in Modern poetry.

16 T. S. Eliot, *The Complete Poems and Plays 1909-1950* (New York: Harcourt, Brace and World, Inc., 1971) 4, 5.
    Note: Further quotes from the above text will be indicated by the contraction *CPE* followed by page numbers in parenthesis.

17 Enid Welsford, *The Fool: His Social and Literary History* (Gloucester, Mass.: Peter Smith, 1966) 239.

18 M. L. Rosenthal and Sally M. Gall, *The Modern Poetic Sequence: The Genius of Modern Poetry* (New York: Oxford University Press, 1983) 160.

19 Constantine FitzGibbon, ed., *Selected Letters of Dylan Thomas* (London: J. M. Dent and Sons Ltd., 1966) 85.

20 David Holbrook, *Dylan Thomas: The Code of Night* (London: The Athlone Press, 1972) 11, 35, 36.

21 Constantine FitzGibbon, *The Life of Dylan Thomas* (Boston Little Brown and Co., 1965) 46.

22 Georg M. A. Gaston, *Dylan Thomas: A Reference Guide* (Boston: G. K. Hall and Co., 1987) 171.

23 John Ackerman, *Dylan Thomas: His Life and Work* (London: Oxford University Press, 1964) 37.

24 Dylan Thomas, *The Collected Stories* (New York: New Directions Books, 1971) 239. *Note*: Further quotes from the above text will be indicated by the contraction *CS* followed by page numbers in parenthesis.

25 John Logan, "Dylan Thomas and the Ark of Art," *Critical Essays on Dylan Thomas*, ed. Georg M. A. Gaston (Boston: G. K. Hall, 1989) 43.

26 Dylan Thomas, *The Collected Poems* (New York: New Directions Books, 1957) 2. *Note*: Further quotes from the above text will be indicated by the contraction *CP* followed by page numbers in parenthesis.

27 William Shakespeare, "Twelfth Night," *William Shakespeare: The Complete Works*, ed. Alfred Harbage (New York: The Viking Press, 1969) 334. The clown is a free ranging spirit who can move from the main-plot to the sub-plot and vice versa with impunity. The boys in Dylan Thomas' poem, like the clown, affirm human nature.

28 Ralph Maud, ed., *The Notebooks of Dylan Thomas* (New York: New Directions, 1967) 98.

29 William York Tindall, *A Reader's Guide to Dylan Thomas* (New York: Octagon Books, 1973) 43-44.

30 Richard A. Davies, "Dylan Thomas' Image of the 'Young Dog' in the Portrait," *The Anglo-Welsh Review* 26.58 (Spring 1977): 68.

31 Vernon Watkins, ed., *Dylan Thomas: Letters to Vernon Watkins* (New York: New Directions Books, 1957) 27.

32 Kenneth Seib, *"Portrait of the Artist as a Young Dog: Dylan's Dubliners,"* *Critical Essays on Dylan Thomas*, ed. Georg M. A. Gaston (Boston: G. K. Hall and Co., 1989) 144.

33 Andrew Sinclair, *Dylan Thomas: No Man More Magical* (New York: Holt, Rinehart and Winston, 1975) 42. The poem is also partly quoted in Paul Ferris' *Dylan Thomas* (New York: The Dial Press, 1977) 52.

34 H. H. Kleinman, *The Religious Sonnets of Dylan Thomas* (Berkeley: University of California Press, 1963) 16.

35 David Clay Jenkins, "Shrine of the Boily Boy: The Dylan Thomas Notebooks at Buffalo," *The Anglo-Welsh Review* 19.43 (Autumn 1970): 119-20.

36 Dylan Thomas, *Under Milk Wood* (New York: Simon and Schuster, 1972) 85.

37 FitzGibbon, *Life* 57, 311; Paul Ferris, *Dylan Thomas* (New York: The Dial Press, 1977) 247. Ferris quotes Moffat commenting on the likeness between Dylan Thomas and Charles Chaplin: "They were roughly the same size...and both possessed this extremely fluid rag-doll like, quick emotion, striding about the enormous drawing-room together, talking and chattering."

38 E. E. Cummings, "Him," *Three Plays and a Ballet*, ed. George J. Firmage (London: Peter Owen, 1968) 11.

Conclusion

Hopkins, Thompson, and Johnson, each in his own way concerned himself with the panorama of the human self in conflict with itself and the divine force. In the milieu of religious and scientific disputations, of man's disaffection with his environment, both outer and inner, these poets employed what John Tyndall in another context referred to as "various modes of leverage" in order to "raise life to a higher level."[1] Aware of the power of their own inner visions, they celebrated their adopted religion, Catholicism, as the mark of unity in an otherwise chaotic existence. Each of the poets set the goal of priesthood as his vocation in life, with varying sense of fulfilment. Hopkins became a Jesuit priest, achieving what he had prepared himself for, but he was never relieved of the immense responsibilities and heart-aches the vocation demanded of him—a human figure torn by illness, exhaustion, and constant self-reminder of his own slim poetic output. Francis Thompson studied for the priesthood only to be disappointed by the decision of the President of Ushaw College, who wrote to his father:

> He has always been a remarkably docile and obedient boy, and certainly one of the cleverest boys in his class. Still, his strong, nervous timidity has increased to such an extent that I have been most reluctantly compelled to concur in the opinion of his Director and others that it is not the holy will of God that he should go on for the Priesthood.[2]

But Thompson expressed in his poetry his enthusiasm and faith in the Catholic tradition. Lionel Johnson constantly referred to becoming a priest even at the early age of seventeen, as evidenced in his letter to J. H. Badley, written on 10 May 1884:

> I will be a priest of the Church of England....Only think of the chances which the priesthood offers: the countless influences of the pulpit and the altar, all potent against the devil in even feeble hands: and how I could train myself![3]

He, however, never realized his early ideal. In his yearnings for a spiritual order—a kind of Paterian "hieratic beauty"—Johnson converted to Catholicism and confirmed for himself that life is a ceremony and a ritual.[4] Thus, each of the poets, Hopkins, Thompson, and Johnson found through his own effort an artistic rendering of his vocational ideal—a rendering not free of inner turmoil and self-laceration but also not bereft of a significant response to living on the brink of a century's final death throes. Hopkins, Thompson, and Johnson responded to the possibility of the death of God by the self's renewed assertion of a resurrected faith. The present study, emphasizing the poet-text-reader interactions, examined how specifically the poets differ in the way they handle human dilemmas at the crossroads of the earthly and the divine. It also studied how the poets direct their movement to success through failure, and how their personae's sufferings, doubts and anxieties about the self's failures serve as straining, but necessary, directives for the final inscapes and visions of God.

The greater possibilities of individualizing the textual perspectives in Hopkins' poems prefigure the endeavors of the moderns. Although Hopkins differed from the moderns in projecting a religious certitude in his poems, the drama (both within the persona and in his interaction with the reader) takes precedence over any referential statements. The first two chapters concentrate on exposing the enactment of this drama in the context of self's struggle with different kinds of failure. In Francis Thompson and Lionel Johnson, however, the personae's perspectives are often aligned to a theologically confirmed viewpoint or an aesthetically defined convention; resolution rather than conflict becomes the dominant thrust of the personae, yet this resolution results in a metaphysical disjunction in an age of conflicting socio-political and economic programs and agendas.

The study of the textual perspectives and their interactions extends to the modern poets in the fifth chapter. The beginning of Modernism was not marked by an immediately discernible demarcation. The *fin de siècle* mood continued into the twentieth century. Only now the historical turns and tides, which had been the source of disaffection among the decadents, became much more pronounced and could no longer be evaded—the von Hartmann interest in the unconscious reached a fully developed psychoanalytical theory in Freud; British imperialism met defeat at the Boer wars; Christian discourse underwent increasing shifts since "secularism, positivism, Marxism and Fabian socialism were competing to be the most effective means of articulation and explaining society" as well as influencing "the working classes."[5] The religious centered world of the Victorians and the art centered one of the decadent aesthetes was countered and often problematized by the concrete images of the *Imagistes*, even as in painting a revolutionary trend towards innovation and individualism found expression in Fauvism, Abstract Impressionism, and Cubism. The Moderns declared themselves free of the circumspection and strait-laced morality of Victorianism. But neither did they feel comfortable to be aesthetes living in an inner world of dreams. If they sought religious faith, they sought it as a direct statement of their own age's tragic search for the tenables; and if they rejected it, they only seemed to affirm the inevitable alienation of "modern man."

With the Moderns, the dilemma was not so much how to relate to God, how to resurrect the self's faith in ultimate goodness or how to celebrate triumph through defeat, but rather how to relate to oneself, how to understand the drive to failure, annihilation, war, atrophy within and without, and how to express the disintegration and fragmentation of self and the world through language that sustains and personae that survive. Alfred Kazin, in "The Posthumous Life of Dylan Thomas," notes how Thomas "felt that life in the twentieth century is peculiarly chaotic and measureless, full of desperate private rebellions and self-blame in a society which less and less gives most people any ideal to be faithful to."[6] Thomas' poems were written, as he himself said, "'in praise of God by a man who doesn't believe in God'—and that only 'the force that through the green fuse drives the flower, the life process from love to death, is real'" (36). The only triumphs that Modern poets claimed were their constant projections of personae (vital, complex, often unexpected, and various) who invigorate the reading process despite their expressions of constant failure. The dramatic context, so appealing to the New Critic (because so full of the possibilities for the interplay of irony, tension, and parody), becomes a medium for reader-involvement. This very medium is used to create a certain kind of reader—alienated, self-critical, and often a self-styled failure; in other words a figure who like the personae in Modern poetry aspires to the role of a clown. This figure of the clown that both the personae and the readers shape into existence is really an image and an act of the mind, inflating and collapsing the substance of self and the world in its infinite bumps and seemingly accidental falls.

ii

Revisiting the arguments that I posited at the beginning of this book, I will provide my closing comments on the process of canonicity, its linkages to politics of neo-imperialism, as well as its manifestations, disguised or otherwise, in late nineteenth and early twentieth century British poets. Scholars like Martin Green, Patrick Brantlinger, Raymond Williams, Fredric Jameson, and Neil Larsen examine these manifestations in fiction, particularly the genre of adventure novels.[6] British poetry of this highly critical phase in British literary and cultural history has been critiqued in terms of its modernist aesthetic practices; the political and ideological crises that they reflected and exposed (particularly with regard to gender, race, class and imperialism), often in self-contradictory images and universalizing myths, have not been subjected to critical study, excepting in a few major figures. In my project I have attempted to bridge this gap. Besides, my attempt is not simply to select writers who most obviously reflect the themes of politically significant ideological struggles, such as Rudyard Kipling, Thomas Love Peacock, John Ruskin, but to examine poets whose works have traditionally been read as "apolitical" or marginally political. On the contrary, my purpose has been to examine the pervasive presence of politically relevant and viable issues, realities, concerns and struggles that underlie their poetry. In doing so, I do not simply disregard previous readings, because I do believe the diverse positionalities of readers will elicit multiple readings. However, I believe my perspective, as a reader who positions herself outside the circumscribed circle of "interpretive communities" or at best at the very embattled nexus of "decolonizing" traditions, as the "unintended reader," reveals new layers of interpretation. Eclectic in my critical practice, I find legitimate grounds for my literary interpretation in various theoretical models, often brought into dialogical play—Reader-Response, New Historicism, Deconstructionism, Feminism, as well as Postcolonialism, in particular have often intersected in my readings and re-readings.

My methodological premises and the thematic development of my book are interlinked processes that examine, even as they perform, the "resistance" motif. The concept of "failure," with all its dialectical implications, in various materialist and ideological contexts and frameworks, has dominated Euro-American literature, from late nineteenth century, in specific ways. In the poetry I examine, "failure" could be seen as a manifestation of "the crisis in representation and agency" that Neil Larsen attributes to "the transformation of 'classical' free market capitalism into monopoly/state capitalism and imperialism" (xxiv) and global multinational capitalism today. It often manifests itself in the form of religious symbolism as human weakness, often as physical versus spiritual dialectic; its philosophical, psychological, socio-economic, and political underpinnings derive from theories ranging from St. Ignatius, Duns Scotus, to Marx, Darwin, Von Hartmann, Freud as well as Western manifestations of non-Western ideologies and practices (Exoticism, Orientalism, Occultism, Cubism, and Transcendentalism) as well as "Liberal reform impulses" represented by James and John Stuart Mill, Bentham and Macaulay, impulses which furthered the cause of the colonial project (Brantlinger 27). Eric Stokes in *The English Utilitarians and India* demonstrates the connection between domestic reform, " the important figures in the intellectual history of English liberalism in the nineteenth century" and imperialism abroad.[7] Patrick Brantlinger expounds on this connection made by Stokes:

> Stokes demonstrates that the articulation between Indian history and the liberal attitudes and movements concerned with domestic reform was both intricate and powerful. Similarly, the movement for the abolition of slavery was also a precursor to the European partitioning of Africa. So the connections between reform at home and empire abroad proliferate. Indeed, it was largely out of the liberal, reform-minded optimism of the early Victorians that the apparently more conservative, social Darwinian, Jingoist imperialism of the late Victorians evolved. (27)

The New Critical rationale for ignoring the "political" nature of the ideologies manifested in High Modernism, however, has been attacked by structural Marxists, cultural materialists, postcolonial and postmodern theorists and critics. The radicalism of Yeats, Eliot, Pound and Lawrence, as well as Conrad has been re-read as aligning itself with "imperialism and fascism" (Brantliger 269). Yeats, however, as nationalist poet has been reclaimed by Edward Said, who declares,

> Nevertheless, and despite Yeats's obvious and, I would say, settled presence in Ireland, in British culture and literature, he does present another fascinating aspect: that of the indisputably great *national* poet who articulates the experiences, the aspirations, and the vision of a people suffering under the dominion of an offshore power.[8]

However, whether Yeats' nationalism complies a stance for decolonization is debatable. Stephen Regan's reading undercuts this perspective. Regan challenges Said's interpretation of Yeats by exploring the contradictions and ambivalences in Yeats' "nationalist ideals":

> The response Yeats makes to the land and the people cannot, then, be considered as a direct act of decolonization since the account of English-Irish relations on which it is based is both ambivalent and evasive. Such a response issues from the insecurity and marginalization of the Anglo-Irish Ascendancy in the face of growing Catholic nationalist aspiration, and not simply from some shared or unified resistance to

English colonial power." (77)

In my reading of Dylan Thomas, I focus not only on his modernist concerns but on issues of his English/Welsh identity, the implications of his rejection of the Swansea moral code while celebrating the Welsh landscape. This preoccupation, with all its complex recreations of space, mapping, geography, local legends, myths, dialect and Welsh practices, connects Thomas to Yeats and Joyce. This connection does not necessarily imply that any one of them can be described, as Edward Said does with Yeats, "nationalist artists of decolonization and revolutionary nationalism, like Tagore, Senghor, Neruda, Vallejo, Cesaire, Faiz, Darwish" (73). While Dylan Thomas did not write as a nationalist poet, the elements of resistance to English imperialism in his writing is often expressed through the construction of a complex persona who combines a self-conscious criticism of nativist sectarianism with an unrestrained celebration of Welsh landscape, dialect and mythography.

The poets I examine are profoundly influenced by notions and events that are often categorized as broad humanistic imperatives. In my study, I explore the nature of poetry as an enactment of a panorama of experiences, observations and feelings both by a poet situated in a concrete historical context as well as a reader whose cultural matrix shapes her/his articulation of poetry. That which becomes meaningful, substantive, significant in the process is the complex ways not only poets, readers and texts interact and interanimate, but the cultural spheres that each inhabits collude, collide or co-exist. The reading process, thus defined, entails any number of interpretive stances and positionalities; however, each must be supported by experiences that are viable not only in dominant cultural domains; they must become forceful and compelling in the marginalized domains, as well as in the intersections of continually reshaping boundary lines among the variously defiend and distributed nodes of privilege and penalty.

Notes

1. John Tyndall, "The Belfast Address," *Science and Religion in the Nineteenth Century*, ed. Tess Cossett (Cambridge: Cambridge University Press, 1984) 186.

2. Everard Meynell, *The Life of Francis Thompson* (London: Burns and Oates, 1913) 32.

3. Sir Francis Russell, ed., *Some Winchester Letters of Lionel Johnson* (London: George Allen and Unwin, 1919) 85-86.

4. Katherine Tynan, *The Middle Years* (London: Constable and Co., 1916) 145.

5. Lynn Hapgood, "Urban Utopias: Socialism, Religion and the City, 1880-1900," *Cultural Politics at the Fin de siècle,* eds. Sally Ledger and Scott McCracken. Cambridge: Cambridge University Press, 1995) 185-186.

6. Alfred Kazin, *"The Posthumous Life of Dylan Thomas,"* ed. Georg Gaston, *Critical Essays on Dylan Thomas* (Boston: G. K. Hall and Co., 1989) 36.

7. Martin Green, *Dreams of Adventure, Deeds of Empire* (New York: Basic Books, 1979; Patrick Brantlinger, *Rule of Darkness: British Literature and Imperialism 1830-1914* (Ithaca: Cornell University Press, 1988); Raymond Williams, *The Politics of Modernism* (London: Verso, 1989); Neil Larsen, *Modernism and Hegemony: A Materialist Critique of Aesthetic Agencies* (Minneapolis: University of Minnesota Press, 1989).

8. Edward W. Said, *Yeats and Decolonization* (Derry: Field Day, 1988) 8. A revised version of this piece appears in *Culture and Imperialism* (London: Chatto and Windus, 1993).

9. Stephen Regan, "W. B. Yeats and Irish Cultural Politics in the 1890s, " *Cultural Politics at the Fin de Siècle,* eds. Sally Ledger and Scott McCracken. Cambridge: Cambridge University Press, 1995) 69, 72.

Bibliography

Primary Sources

Eliot, T. S. *The Complete Poems and Plays 1909-1950*. NewYork: Harcourt, Brace and World, 1971.

Hopkins, G. M. *Further Letters of Gerard Manley Hopkins*. Ed. Claude Colleer Abbott. London: Oxford University Press, 1956.

———.*The Correspondence of Gerard Manley Hopkins and Richard Watson Dixon*. Ed Claude Colleer Abbott. London: Oxford University Press, 1955.

———.*The Journals and Papers of Gerard Manley Hopkins*. Ed. Humphrey House. London: Oxford University Press, 1959.

———.*The Letters of Gerard Manley Hopkins to Robert Bridges*. Ed. Claude Colleer Abbott. London: Oxford University Press, 1955.

———.*The Notebooks and Papers of Gerard Manley Hopkins*.Ed. Humphrey House. London: Oxford Univrsity Press, 1937.

———.*The Poems of Gerard Manley Hopkins*. Ed. W. H. Gardner and N. H. MacKenzie. 4th ed. Oxford: Oxford University Press, 1967.

———.*The Sermons and Devotional Writings of Gerard Manley-Hopkins*. Ed. Christopher Devlin, S. J. London: Oxford University Press, 1959.

Johnson, Lionel. "Incurable." *The Pageant*, I, n.p.1896.

———.*Post Liminium: Essays and Critical Papers*. Ed. Thomas Whittemore. London: E. MaThews, 1911.

———.*Reviews and Critical Papers*. Ed. Robert Schafer. London: Elkin Mathews, 1921.

———.*Some Letters to Richard Le Gallienne*. Edinburgh: Tregara Press, 1979.

———.*Some Winchester Letters of Lionel Johnson*. London: George Allen and Unwin, 1919.

———.*The Art of Thomas Hardy*. London: Elkin Mathews, 1894.

———.*The Collected Poems of Lionel Johnson*. New York: Garland Publishing, 1982.

———.*The Religious Poems of Lionel Johnson*. London: Elkin Mathews, 1916.

Pound, Ezra. *Selected Poems*. New York: New Directions, 1957.

———."Vorticism." *Fortnightly Review*, XCVI, no. 573, Sept. 1914.

Thomas, Dylan. *Dylan Thomas: Letters to Vernon Watkins*. Ed. Vernon Watkins. New York: New Directions, 1957.

———.*Selected Letters of Dylan Thomas*. Ed. Constantine Fitz Gibbon. London: J. M. Dent and Sons, 1966.

———.*The Collected Poems*. New York: New Directions, 1957.

———.*The Collected Stories*. New York: New Directions, 1971.

———.*The Notebooks of Dylan Thomas*. New York: New Directions,

1967.

———.*The Poems of Dylan Thomas*. Ed. Daniel Jones. New York: New Directions, 1971.

———.*Under Milk Wood*. New York: Simon and Schuster, 1972.

Thompson, Francis. *A Renegade Poet and Other Essays*. Freeport, New York: Books for Libraries, 1910.

———.*Francis Thompson: Poems and Essays*. Three Vols. in One. Ed. Wilfrid Meynell. New York: Books for Libraries Press, 1947.

———.*Literary Criticisms*. Ed. Terence L. Connolly. Westport, Conn.: Greenwood Press, 1975.

———.*Minor Poets: Criticisms Newly Discovered and Collected*. Ed. Terence L. Connolly. Los Angeles: Anderson and Ritchie, 1949.

———.*Poems of Francis Thompson*. Ed. Terence L. Connolly. New York: Appleton-Century-Crofts, 1941.

———.*The Letters of Francis Thompson*. Ed. John E. Walsh. New York: Hawthorn Books, 1969.

———.*The Man Has Wings: New Poems and Plays*. Ed. Terence L. Connolly. Garden City, New York: Doubleday and Co., 1957.

Yeats, W. B. *Autobiographies*. London: Macmillan Co., 1955.

———.*Mythologies*. New York: Macmillan Co., 1959.

Yeats, W. B. and Johnson, Lionel. *Poetry and Ireland*. Churchtown: Cuala Press, 1908.

———.*The Collected Poems*. New York: Macmillan Co., 1956.

Secondary Sources

Ackerman, John. *Dylan Thomas: His Life and Work*. London: Oxford University Press, 1964.

———.*Welsh Dylan: Dylan Thomas' Life, Writing, and his Wales*. Cardiff: Jones, 1979.

Allsopp, Michael and David Anthony Downes. *Saving Beauty. Further Studies in Hopkins*. New York: Garland, 1994.

Augustine, St. *The Confessions of St. Augustine*. Transl. J. G. Pilkington. Norwalk, Conn.: The Heritage Press, 1963.

Barrett, William. *The Irrational Man: A Study in Existential Philosophy*. Garden City, New York: Doubleday, 1958.

Beyette, Thomas K. "Hopkins' Phenomenology of Art in 'The Shepherd's Brow'." *Victorian Poetry* 11 (Autumn, 1973): 207-213.

Blunt, Wilfrid Scawan. *My Diaries: Being a Personal Narrative of Events, 1888-1914*. Part One. New York: Alfred A. Knopf, 1921.

Boardman, Brigid M. *Between Heaven and Charing Cross: The Life of Francis Thompson*. New Haven: Yale University Press, 1988.

Bongie, Chris. *Exotic Memories: Literature, Colonialism and the Fin de *siècle*. Stanford: Stanford University Press, 1991.

Booth, Wayne C. *The Rhetoric of Fiction*. Second ed. Chicago: Chicago University Press, 1983.

Boyle S.J., Robert. *Metaphor in Hopkins*. Chapel Hill, 1961.

Brantlinger, Patrick. *Rule of Darkness: British Literature and Imperialism 1830-1914*. Ithaca: Cornell University Press, 1988.

Brinnin, John Malcolm, ed. *A Casebook on Dylan Thomas*. New York: Cromwell, 1960.

———.*Dylan Thomas in America, an Intimate Journal*. Boston: Little, Brown, 1955.

Buss, Arnold H. *Self Consciousness and Social Anxiety*. San Francisco: W. H. Freeman and Co., 1980.

Campbell, Sr. M. Mary Hugh. "The Silent Sonnet: Hopkins' 'Shepherd's Brow'." *Renascence* 15 (Spring 1963): 133-142.

Chai, Leon. *Aestheticism: The Religion of Art in Post-Romantic Literature*. New York: Columbia University Press, 1990.

Charlesworth, Barbara. *Dark Passages: the Decadent Consciousness in Victorian Literature*. Madison, Wisconsin: University of Wisconsin Press, 1965.

Chevigny, Bell Gale. "Instress and Devotion in the Poetry of Gerard Manley Hopkins." *Victorian Studies* 9 (1965): 141-153.

Chinweizu, et al. *Toward the Decolonization of African Literature*. Enugu, Nigeria: Fourth Dimension, 1980.

Clark, S. J., Robert Boykin. "Hopkins's 'The Shepherd's Brow.'" *Victorian Newsletter* 28 (Fall 1965): 16-18.

Clifton, Gerald Kent. *"Lost in Light": A Study of Lionel Johnson's Poetry*. Diss. University of California, Irvine 1978.

Connolly, Terence L. *Francis Thompson: In his Paths, a Visit to Persons and Places Associated With the Poet*. Milwaukee: The Bruce Publishing Co., 1914.

———."Laudanum or Poetry?" *Renascence* 13 (Summer 1961): 200-206.

Cotter, James Finn. *Inscape: The Christology and Poetry of Gerard.Manley Hopkins*. Pittsburgh: University of Pittsburgh Press, 1972.

Cox, C. B. *Dylan Thomas, a Collection of Critical Essays*. Englewood Cliffs, New Jersey: Prentice-Hall, 1966.

Cummings, E. E. "Him." *Three Plays and a Ballet*. Ed. George J. Firmage. London: Peter Owen, 1968.

Davies, Aneirin Talfan. *Dylan: Druid of the Broken Body*. London: J. M. Dent, 1964.

Davies, Richard A. "Dylan Thomas's Image of the 'Young Dog' in the Portrait." *The Anglo-Welsh Review* 26.58 (Spring 1977):68-72.

Davies, Walford, ed. *Dylan Thomas: New Critical Essays*. London: Dent, 1972.

Dowling, Linda C. "Pursuing Antithesis: Lionel Johnson on Hardy." *English Language Notes* 12: 4 (June 1975): 287-292.

———."The Decadent and the New Woman." *Nineteenth Century Fiction* 33 (1979): 440-441.

———.*Language and Decadence in the Victorian Fin de Siècle*. Princeton: Princeton University Press, 1986.

Downes, David Anthony. *Hopkins' Achieved Self.* Lanham, Maryland: University Press of America, 1996.

———."A Readers' Life: Selving Through Reading Hopkins" in Allsopp and Downes. ed. 327-343.

Dykstra, Bram. *Idols of Perversity: Fantasies of Feminine Evil in Fin de Siècle Culture*. New York: Oxford University Press, 1986.

Eble, Joseph. "Levels of Awareness: A Reading of Hopkins' 'Felix Randal'." *Victorian Poetry* 13 (1975): 131-132.

Ellmann, Richard. *Yeats: The Man and His Masks*. New York: E. P. Dutton and Co., 1948.

Emeka, Okeke-Ezigbo. "The 'Sharp and Sided Hail': Hopkins and the Nigerian Imitators and Detractors." *Hopkins Among the Poets: Studies in Modern Responses to Gerard Manley Hopkins*. Ed. Richard F. Giles. Hamilton, Ontario: The International Hopkins Association Monograph Series, 1985: 114-123.

Empson, William. *Seven Types of Ambiguity*. London: Chatto and Windus, 1930.

Fanon, Frantz. *Black Skin, White Masks*. New York: Grove Press, 1967.

———.*The Wretched of the Earth*. New York: Grove Press, 1968.

Faverty, Frederic Everett, ed. *The Victorian Poets: a Guide to Research*. Cambridge: Harvard University Press, 1968.

Fennell, Francis L., ed. *The Fine Delight: Centenary Essays on Gerard Manley Hopkins*. Chicago: Loyola University Press, 1989.

Ferris, Paul. *Dylan Thomas*. New York: The Dial Press, 1977.

Fish, Stanley. *Is There a Text in This Class? The Authority of Interpretive Communities*. Cambridge: Harvard University Press, 1980.

FitzGibbon, Constantine. *The Life of Dylan Thomas*. Boston: Little Brown, 1965.

Gallienne, Richard Le. *The Romantic '90s*. Garden City, New York: Doubleday, Page and Co., 1926.

Gardner, W. H. *Gerard Manley Hopkins (1844-1889): A Study of Poetic Idiosyncrasy in Relation to Poetic Tradition*. Vols. I and II. New Haven: Yale University Press, 1948, 1949.

Gaston, Georg. *Dylan Thomas: A Reference Guide*. Boston: G. K. Hall, 1987.

———.*Critical Essays on Dylan Thomas*. Boston: G. K. Hall, 1989.

Gilbert, Sandra M. and Susan Gubar. *The Madwoman in the Attic: The Woman Writer and the Nineteenth Century Literary Imagination*. New

Haven: Yale University Press, 1979.

———.*No Man's Land: Place of the Woman Writer in the Twentieth Century*. Vols. 1 and 2. New Haven: Yale University Press, 1988.

Giles, Richard F. *Hopkins Among the Poets: Studies in Modern Responses to Gerard Manley Hopkins*. Hamilton, Ontario: The International Hopkins Association, 1985.

Green, Martin. *Dreams of Adventure, Deeds of Empire*. New York: Basic Books, 1979.

Harbage, Alfred. *William Shakespeare: The Complete Works*. New York: The Viking Press, 1969.

Hart, Dominick "The Experience of Dylan Thomas' Poetry." *The Anglo-Welsh Review* 26.58 (Spring 1977): 73-78.

Holbrook, David. *Dylan Thomas: The Code of Night*. London: The Athlone Press, 1972.

———.*Llareqqub Revisited: Dylan Thomas and the State of Modern Poetry*. London: Bowes and Bowes, 1962.

Hollahan, Eugene. *Hopkins Against History*. New York: Creighton University Press, 1995.

Holub, Robert C. *Reception Theory: A Critical Introduction*. New York: Methuen, 1984.

Honnïghausen, Lothar. *The Symbolist Tradition in English Literature: A Study of Pre-Raphaelitism and Fin de Siècle*. Transl. Gisela

Honnighausen. Cambridge: Cambridge University Press, 1988 (1971).

Iser, Wolfgang. *The Act of Reading: A Theory of Aesthetic Response*. Baltimore: The Johns Hopkins University Press, 1978.

——.*The Implied Reader: Patterns of Communication in Prose Fiction from Bunyan to Beckett*. Baltimore: The Johns Hopkins University Press, 1974.

Jenkins, David C. "Shrine of the Boily Boy: The Dylan Thomas Notebooks at Buffalo." *Anglo-Welsh Review* 19.43 (Autumn 1970): 114-129.

Johnson, Wendell Stacy. "Sexuality and Inscape." *The Hopkins Quarterly* 3.2 (July 1976):59-65.

Jones, Daniel. *My Friend Dylan Thomas*. London: Dent, 1977.

Kazin, Alfred. "The Posthumous Life of Dylan Thomas." *Critical Essays on Dylan Thomas*. Ed. Georg Gaston. Boston: G.K. Hall, 1989.

Kenner, Hugh. *The Pound Era*. Berkeley: University of California Press, 1971.

Kerr, Walter. *Tragedy and Comedy*. New York: Simon and Schuster, 1967.

Kidder, Rushworth M. *Dylan Thomas: The Country of the Spirit*. Princeton, New Jersey: Princeton University Press, 1973.

Kitchen, Paddy. *Gerard Manley Hopkins*. New York: Atheneum, 1979.

Kleinman, Hyman H. *The Religious Sonnets of Dylan Thomas: A Study in Imagery and Meaning*. Berkeley: University of California Press, 1963.

Krishnamurti, G., ed. *The Hound of Heaven: A Commemorative Volume.* London: Francis Thompson Society, 1967.

Laclau, Ernesto and Chantal Mouffe. *Hegemony and Socialist Strategy: Towards a Radical Democratic Politics.* London: Verso, 1985.

Larsen, Neil. *Modernism and Hegemony: A Materialist Critique of Aesthetic Agencies.* Minneapolis: University of Minnesota Press, 1989.

Lawrence, Karen R. *Decolonizing Tradition: New Visions of Twentieth-Century "British" Literary Canons.* Urbana: University of Illinois Press, 1992.

Le Buffe, S. J., Francis. *"The Hound of Heaven": An Interpretation.* New York: The Macmillan Co., 1921.

Lewis, C. Day. *The Poetic Image.* London: Oxford University Press, 1947.

Logan, John. "Dylan Thomas and the Ark of Art." *Critical Essays on Dylan Thomas.* Ed. Georg Gaston. Boston: G.K. Hall, 1989. 42-49.

Loyola, St. Ignatius. *The Spiritual Exercises.* Transl. L. Fleming, S. J. St. Louis: The Institute of Jesuit Sources, 1978.

Lyotard, Francois. *The Postmodern Condition.* Minneapolis: University of Minnesota Press, 1984.

MacKenzie, Norman H. *A Reader's Guide to Gerard Manley Hopkins.* Ithaca: Cornell University Press, 1981.

Mariani, Paul L. "The artistic and Tonal Integrity of Hopkins' 'The Shepherd's Brow'." *Victorian Poetry* 6 (Spring 1968): 63-68.

———."The Sound of oneself Breathing: The Burden of Theological Metaphor in Hopkins." *The Hopkins Quarterly* 4:1 (Spring 1977).

Martin, Robert Bernard. *Gerard Manley Hopkins: A Very Private Life*. London: Harper Collins, 1991.

Maud, Ralph. *Dylan Thomas in Print, a Bibliographical History*. Pittsburgh: University of Pittsburgh Press, 1970.

———. *Entrances to Dylan Thomas' Poetry*. Pittsburgh: University of Pittsburgh, 1963.

McNabb, Rev. Vincent Joseph. *Francis Thompson, and other Essays*. Freeport, New York: Books for Libraries Press, 1936.

Megroz, Rodolphe Louis. *Francis Thompson: The Poet of Earth Heaven; a Study in Poetic Mysticism and the Evolution of Love-Poetry*. New York: Scribner, 1927.

Meynell, Viola. *Francis Thompson and Wilfrid Meynell, a Memoir*. London: Hollis and Carter, 1952.

Meynell, Everard. *The Life of Francis Thompson*. London: Burns and Oates, 1913.

Miller, J. Hillis. "The Theme of the Disappearance of God in Victorian Poetry." *Victorian Studies* 6 (Mar. 1963):207-227.

Morris, James. *Pax Britannica: The Climax of an Empire*. New York: Harcourt, Brace and World, 1968.

Motto, Mary Lou. *Mined With a Motion: The Poetry of Gerard Manley*

Hopkins. New Jersey: Rutgers University Press, 1984.

Moynihan, William T. *The Craft and Art of Dylan Thomas*. Ithaca: Cornell University Press, 1966.

Myerly, Scott Hughes. "The Eye Must Entrap the Mind: Army Spectacle and Paradigm in Nineteenth-Century Britain." *Journal of Social History* 26.1 (Fall 1992): 105-132.

Nelles, William. "Historical and Implied Authors and Readers." *Comparative Literature* 45.1 (1993): 22-47.

O'Connor, Rev. John. *"The Mistress of Vision" by FrancisThompson*. London: Saint Albert's Press, 1966.

Pater, Walter. *Marius the Epicurean: His Sensations and Ideas*. London: Macmillan and Co., 1910.

Peters, W. A. M. *Gerard Manley Hopkins: A Critical Essay Towards the Understanding of his Poetry*. New York: Oxford University Press, 1948.

Phare, Elsie Elizabeth. *The Poetry of Gerard Manley Hopkins*. New York: Russell and Russell, 1933.

Pick, John. *Gerard Manley Hopkins: Poet and Priest*. London: Oxford University Press, 1966.

Pierrot, Jean. *The Decadent Imagination 1880-1900*. Transl. Derek Coltman. Chicago: University of Chicago Press, 1981.

Pope, Myrtle Pihlman. *A Critical Bibliography of Works By and About*

Francis Thompson. Folcroft, Penn.: Folcroft Library Editions, 1972.

Read, Herbert. *Form in Modern Poetry*. London: Sheed and Ward, 1932.

Regan, Stephen. "W. B. Yeats and Irish Cultural Politics in the 1890s" *Cultural Politics at the Fin de Siècle*. Eds. Sally Ledger and Scott McCracken. Cambridge: Cambridge University Press, 1995.

Reid, John C. *Francis Thompson: Man and Poet*. London: Routledge and Kegan Paul, 1959.

Richards, I. A. *Practical Criticism*. London: Routledge and Kegan Paul, 1929.

Riggan, William. *Picaros, Madmen, Naifs, and Clowns: The Unreliable First-Person Narrator*. Norman: University of Oklahoma Press, 1981.

Robinson, John. *In Extremity: A Study of Gerard Manley Hopkins*. Cambridge: Cambridge University Press, 1978.

Rolph, John Alexander. *Dylan Thomas, a Bibliography*. London: Dent, 1956.

Rorty, Richard. *Consequences of Pragmatism (Essays: 1972-1980)*. Minneapolis: University of Minnesota Press, 1982.

Rosenblatt, Louise M. *The Reader, the Text, the Poem: The Transactional Theory of the Literary Work*. Carbondale: Southern Illinois University Press, 1978.

Rosenthal, M. L. and Gall, Sally M. *The Modern Poetic Sequence: The Genius of Modern Poetry*. New York: Oxford University Press, 1983.

Rothenstein, Sir William. *Men and Memories: Recollections 1872-1938.* Ed. Mary Lago. Columbia: University of Missouri Press, 1978.

Ruskin, John. "Stones of Venice." *Works 8.* London: G. Allen, 1903.

Russell, Lord Francis. *My Life and Adventures.* London, 1923.

Russett, Cynthia Eagle. *Sexual Science: The Victorian Construction of Womanhood.* Cambridge: Harvard University Press, 1989.

Rutenberg, Daniel. "Crisscrossing the Bar: Tennyson and Lionel Johnson on Death." *Victorian Poetry* 10 (Summer 1972):179-180.

Ruthven, K. K. *A Guide to Ezra Pound's "Personae."* Berkeley: University of California Press, 1969.

Said, Edward W. *The World, the Text, and the Critic.* Cambridge: Harvard University Press, 1983.

———.*Yeats and Decolonization.* Derry: Field Day, 1988.

Salmon, Arthur Edward. *Poets of the Apocalypse.* Boston: Twayne, 1983.

Santayana, George. *The Middle Span.* London: Constable, 1947.

Schneider, Elizabeth W. *The Dragon in the Gate: Studies in the Poetry of G. M. Hopkins.* Berkeley: University of California Press, 1968.

Schopenhauer. *Pensees, Maximes et Fragments.* Transl. Burdeau. Paris: Bailliere, 1880.

Seib, Kenneth. *"Portrait of the Artist as a Young Dog: Dylan's Dubliners".*

Critical Essays. Gaston, ed. 139-147.

Showalter, Elaine. *Sexual Anarchy: Gender and Culture at the Fin de Siècle*. New York: Viking, 1990.

———.*Daughters of Decadence: Women Writers of the Fin de Siècle*. New Brunswick, N.J.: Rutgers University Press, 1993.

Sinclair, Andrew. *Dylan Thomas: No Man More Magical*. New York: Holt, Rinehart and Winston, 1975.

Spivak, Gayatri Chakravorti. *In Other Worlds: Essays in Cultural Politics*. New York: Routledge, 1988 (1987).

Stein, Jess, ed. *The Random House College Dictionary*, rev. ed. New York: Random House, 1979.

Sulloway, Alison. *Gerard Manley Hopkins and the Victorian Temper*. New York: Columbia University Press, 1972.

———."Hopkins, Male and Female, and the 'Tender Mothering Earth'." *The Fine Delight: Centenary Essays on Gerard Manley Hopkins*. Ed. Francis L. Fennell. Chicago: Loyola University Press, 1989, 33-54.

Sutherland, John. "'Tom's Garland': Hopkins' Political Poem." *Victorian Poetry* 10 (1972): 111-121.

Templeman, William D. *Bibliographies of Studies in Victorian Literature, 1932-1944*. Urbana: University of Illinois Press, 1945.

The Holy Bible. Authorized King James Version. Oxford: Oxford, University Press.

Thesing, William B. "'Tom's Garland' and Hopkins' Inscapes of Humanity." *Victorian Poetry* 15 (Spring 1977):37-48.

Thomson, John. *Francis Thompson: Poet and Mystic*. New York: Haskell House, 1974.

Thomson, Paul van Kuykendall. *Francis Thompson: A Critical Biography*. New York: Nelson, 1961.

Thornton, R. K. R. *The Decadent Dilemma*. London: Edward Arnold, 1983.

Tindall, William York. *A Reader's Guide to Dylan Thomas*. New York: Farrar, Straus and Cudahy, 1962.

Tobias, Richard C. "Guide to the Year's Work in Victorian Poetry: 1983. General Materials." *Victorian Poetry* 22. 3 (Autumn 1984).279-284.

Treece, Henry. *Dylan Thomas, "dog among the Fairies."* New York: John de Graff, 1956.

Tynan, Katherine. *The Middle Years*. London: Constable and Co., 1916.

Tyndall, John. "The Belfast Address." *Science and Religion in the Nineteenth Century*. Ed. Tess Cosslett. Cambridge: Cambridge University Press, 1984.186.

Wain, John. "An Idiom of Desperation." *Hopkins: A Collection of Critical.Essavs*. Ed. Geoffrey H. Hartman. New Jersey: Prentice-Hall, 1966.

Walhout, Donald. *Send My Roots Rain*. Athens: Ohio University Press,

1981.

Walsh, John E. *Strange Harp, Strange Symphony: The Life of Francis Thompson*. New York: Hawthorn Books, 1967.

Warren, Austin. *Rage for Order*. Chicago: Chicago University Press, 1948.

Waugh, Patricia. *Practising Postmodernism/Reading Modernism*. New York: Edward Arnold, 1992.

Welsford, Enid. *The Fool: His Social and Literary History*. Gloucester, Mass.: Peter Smith, 1966.

Weyand, Norman, ed. *Immortal Diamond: Studies in Gerard Manley Hopkins*. London: Sheed and Ward, 1949.

Wheatley-Lovoy, Cynthia D. "'The Silver Laughter of Wisdom': Joyce, Yeats, and Heroic Farce." *South Atlantic Review* 58.4 (Nov. 1993): 19-37.

Williams, George G. "Thompson's 'Grace of the Way'." *The Explicator* 9.2 (1950):16-17.

Williams, Raymond. *The Politics of Modernism: Against the New Conformists*. Ed. Tony Pinkney. London: Verso, 1989.

Wright, Austin. *Bibliographies of Studies in Victorian Literature 1945-54*. Urbana: University of Illinois Press, 1956.

Pushpa Naidu Parekh is Assistant Professor of English at Spelman College, Atlanta, Georgia. A United States citizen born in India, she received her M.A. from the University of Madras, her M. Phil. from Panjab University, and her Ph.D. from Louisiana State University. Her publications include creative writing and chapters and articles on Indian postcolonial and comparative literature, and a forthcoming reference volume, *Postcolonial African Writers*.